Adulting 101 is a must-read book for anyone, whether you are just entering the "real world" or have been in it for decades. The timeless principles shared by Josh and Pete will have you referencing the book for years to come.

—Andy Stanley, author, communicator, and founder of North Point Ministries

I love meeting young leaders who are eager to change the world. In their new book, *Adulting 101*, Josh Burnette and Pete Hardesty provide a much needed, practical guide for the next generation of world changers. Their inside out approach to personal change will inspire readers to cultivate a growth mindset essential for success in life.

—Dan T. Cathy, Chairman and CEO, Chick-fil-A, Inc.

It seems that some of the practical things an aspiring adult needs to know, like how to create a personal budget, interview for a job, or even take out a loan to buy a car are left to the "learn as you go" educational model. Josh Burnette and Pete Hardesty are out to change that with this fantastic and insightful new book, *Adulting 101*. It is a great book and a useful resource for anyone trying to figure out some of the basics of being on their own.

—Governor Mike Huckabee, best-selling author and political commentator

In *Adulting 101*, Josh Burnette and Pete Hardesty share practical, accessible, and authentic wisdom to help students navigate the transition from college to their lives as independent adults. This is a resource young adults can return to over and over again for advice.

—Jonathan R. Alger, President, James Madison University

Adulting 101 is a practical guide for one of the most exciting times in a person's life. Josh and Pete have captured decades of experience and written a book every young person should read. Read it and apply what you learn. You'll get a ten-year head start on adulthood!

—Mark Miller, best-selling author and speaker

I wish every young person would read this book! Whoever does and takes it to heart will be much more likely to lead a successful life. Warning: Pete and Josh have packed so much great advice and wisdom into this book—you will need to refer to it often to realize the full benefit.

—James M. Herr, Chairman, Herr Foods, Inc.

Adulting 101 is a hole-in-one! I wish I had this essential guide for adult life before I started competing on the tour. This book will help you build a world-class career and become personally fulfilled. If you are in your twenties, read this book! It is a game-changer. *Adulting 101* should top the reading list for any graduate, parent, college student, or anyone working with adolescents.

—Brittany Lincicome, LPGA champion, @Brittany1golf

Pete and Josh know high school and college students very well, and they've written a book that tackles dozens of topics important to becoming an adult. I'm very impressed and encourage those who are "adulting" to read what these authors have written.

—Denny Rydberg, President Emeritus, Young Life

Adulting 101 is a practical and engaging guide on how to live an intentional life that leaves the world a better place than you knew it before. It's both pragmatic and visionary and will help set young adults on a trajectory to live an extraordinary life.

—Ellie Holcomb, Dove Award-winning singer and songwriter

Are you between sixteen and twenty-nine years old? If so, *Adulting 101* is a must-read—engaging and powerfully practical. If you follow the principles provided on its pages, you will increase your chances of being successful by 1,000 percent or even more. *This* is the book I wish someone had given me at that important age!

—Michael Licona, PhD, Associate Professor of Theology,
Houston Baptist University

Adulting 101 is Real Talk. Learn from it. You'll be glad you did. Apply its advice and you will be killing it, especially with what is most important in life. Maximum impact begins on a solid foundation, which you'll find in this book.

—Mark Cathy, Chick-fil-A Inc., Operator Support and Cathy family member

Where was this when I started "adulting"? Pete and Josh lay out a road map for navigating life. *Adulting 101* should be required reading for every twentysomething, but it may be just as valuable for seasoned adults who need a refresher on some of life's important truths. It's like a life manual in your pocket.

—Dave Alpern, President, Joe Gibbs Racing

Pete and Josh really know the relevant issues for college graduates, and they tackle each of these with wisdom clearly borne from years of experience. I'm going to recommend this book to my students and to my own children.

—Lee Coppock, PhD, Professor of Economics, Director of Undergraduate Studies,
Economics Department, University of Virginia

Adulting 101 is a great resource for young people who are getting started in the real world. This book will help you launch into adulthood successfully, and it is relevant for every stage of life because it is principle-based. I believe *Adulting 101* will be and should be read repeatedly, even by those in their "later" years.

—Ron Blue, author and Ronald Blue & Co. founder

As a leader in the US Army for the past twenty years, I have dedicated my life to transforming teenagers into the future leaders of our country. *Adulting 101* contains very practical advice and vignettes to help our teenagers make a successful transition from our homes and into the world. I plan to use what I learned from *Adulting 101* with my two teenagers.

—Col. Eric Lopez, US Army Ranger

Whatever you are currently experiencing in the crazy transitions of life, there is something in this book for you. This book has been a tremendous help transitioning to life on my own. You are not alone, and you can thrive. #LiveYourBestLife with #Adulting101.

—Jess Demayo, recent college graduate

Too many people complain that kids today have a hard time growing up. Well, it's time we step up and help them out. *Adulting 101* is a great book! Buy it for every high school junior or senior you know!

—Chap Clark, PhD, author of *Hurt 2.0: Inside the World of Today's Teenagers*

This powerful book is a must-read for helping people transition to a fulfilling and meaningful adulthood. *Adulting 101* is a handbook filled with gems of practical tips and techniques. Pete and Josh are truly life teachers sharing from their hearts, souls, minds, and spirits.

—Mark Warner, Senior Vice President for Student Affairs,
James Madison University

If you know a young person who is moving into the adult world, or if you know someone who is already in the adult world and floundering, then *Adulting 101* will move you in a direction of fulfillment and success. I'm in the sunset years of life, and I found it to be a practical and fascinating read, even for me.

—Ken Davis, communication trainer, speaker, author, and grandpa

Pete has been a mentor to me for over twenty years. He's had a profound impact on my life and leadership. In *Adulting 101*, Pete and Josh share their own experiences as they present practical wisdom for the journey of life. As a former military officer and current entrepreneur, I recommend this book to all aspiring leaders.

—Brett Gibson, Co-founder and Managing Partner at NextGen Venture Partners

In my forty-plus years of working with young people all over the world, this is one of the best resources I've seen to prepare adolescents for real life. *Adulting 101* is a comprehensive guide to success after school. If you're between the ages of sixteen and twenty-nine, this book could become one of your most important life mentors if you simply read and apply this book like your life depends on it, because it does.

—Dr. Lee Corder, NFL Chaplain Emeritus and Global Youth Mentorship Associate

In a culture where helicopter parenting has become the norm, this is a must-read for anyone who doesn't want to be living in their parents' basement at age twenty-nine.

—Drew Miller, middle school principal

In *Adulting 101*, Josh Burnette and Pete Hardesty offer a comprehensive, practical guide to young adults to help them navigate decisions in ways that will pay dividends in the years ahead.

—Mark A. Yarhouse, PsyD, Rosemarie S. Hughes Endowed Chair
and Professor of Psychology, Regent University

I wish *Adulting 101* was written fifty years ago when I graduated. This book would have helped me become a better student and a better person in general—a better husband, parent, pastor, college professor, and dean. I highly recommend this book.

—Dr. Alex Awad, former Dean of Students, Bethlehem Bible College, Palestine, Israel

Filled with practical insight that high school and college students will have wanted to know ten years from today. Timely and actionable, *Adulting 101* sets out the basics for winning in all spheres of life.

—Kyle Winey, college hacker, author of *HACKiversity*, #1 Amazon best-seller

Over the last twenty years, Pete has helped thousands of young people (including me) navigate our increasingly complex culture by helping them to identify their purpose and their priorities. *Adulting 101* is an invaluable resource to young adults who are finding their way in this world.

—Danny T. K. Avula, MD, MPH, Public Health Director, City of Richmond, VA;
Chair, Virginia State Board of Social Services

This might just be the single most important thing a twentysomething could read.

—Landon Dermott, recent college graduate

If you wonder what's coming in the transition to the real world, this is the book for you. Josh and Pete have captured many of the basic principles that your parents thought you knew.

—Howard Griffith, PhD, Academic Dean and Professor of Systematic Theology,
Reformed Theological Seminary, Washington, DC

After over twenty years on a campus, Pete Hardesty knows how to meet students right where they are. The straightforward wisdom, life skills, and practical revelations shared in *Adulting 101* will undoubtedly benefit those graduating and heading out to launch into life.

—Nick Langridge, Vice President for University Advancement, James Madison University

I wish Josh and Pete had written *Adulting 101* five years ago. I am confident my life would have been much easier. They give us guidance for overcoming nearly anything life throws at you.

—S. Martin, singer and songwriter

I have observed Pete and Josh firsthand connect powerfully with young adults. This book is a must-read for every college senior and graduate seeking to walk in wisdom in their relationships, work, and finances.

—Kristina Doubet, PhD, Professor of Education at James Madison University;
author of *Differentiation in Middle and High School:
Strategies to Engage All Learners* (ASCD)

This book is one of the best guides for a young person starting their journey that I've ever seen —especially if you want significant financial success. Read this book ASAP.

— Michael Basile, CEO at The Summit Investment Group

Pete has been my close friend and mentor for over twenty years. I am so excited that so many others will have the opportunity to benefit from this book and Pete's wisdom, which has been transformative in my life. This is a must-read for those embarking on the great adventure of adulthood.

—Romesh Wijesooriya, Assistant Professor of Pediatrics,
Division Chair of General Pediatrics, Children's Hospital of Richmond
at Virginia Commonwealth University

As an NFL player I'd have done well to have a resource like this book!

—J. Todd Peterson, NFL Placekicker 1993–2006; Chairman, Pro Athletes Outreach

Every now and then you meet someone that you respect and trust because what they say comes from being in the trenches of life with people. Pete is one of those people for me. I wholeheartedly recommend this book to any aspiring leader.

—Pat Goodman, Director of Men's Ministry,
Grace Fellowship Church, Baltimore, MD

Take these tips in *Adulting 101*, and you can't go wrong. This book is a map for navigating life after school and a how-to manual for extreme success. Josh and Pete will help you grow up.

—Rafa Campos, professional golfer

Pete uses his wide experience as a leader of youth to write on subjects close to the heart of teenagers.

—Botrus Mansour, General Director of Nazareth Baptist School, Nazareth, Israel

Pete and Josh ask the right questions and tackle them head on. The book is not just for emerging adults but for parents, teachers, coaches, ministers, and all who want the next generation to become world changers.

—Mike Gaffney, Vice President, Young Life College and University

I quickly learned upon graduating college that I lacked some of the necessary tools to help me succeed in the real world. *Adulting 101* equipped me with life skills that are essential for adulthood and helped launch me. It is funny, relevant, and essential for the young adult who is wondering how to live a life that matters.

—Kelsey Swift, recent college graduate

I've had the privilege of knowing Pete for nearly twenty years. This book, which I consumed in one sitting, gives intensely practical advice for every young collegian to digest. This book will help the reader avoid countless heartbreaks. I predict it will be a blessing to countless young people. I intend to give it to my twenty-year-old son.

—Dan Flynn, Director of Theological Development, Great Lakes Region, Cru

This book is practical, easy to understand, and totally profound all at the same time. As a supervisor to many millennials, I would make this required reading.

—Lawson McNeil, founder, Blue Sky Fund

Adulting 101 is a gift to all graduates. It's the map you've been looking for. Whether it's getting a job, navigating relationships, or understanding the complexity of budgeting and insurance, *Adulting 101* offers a feast of wisdom in bite-sized portions.

—Drew Hill, author of "Alongside: Loving Teenagers with the Gospel" and editor of "The Young Life Leader Blog"

Most people only turn the corner into adulthood once. Pete's done it countless times as he's devoted his life to developing college students into mature men and women. His wisdom is a treasured resource for emerging adults and those who mentor them.

—C. J. Goeller, Intervarsity Campus Director, James Madison University

Adulting 101 is packed with thoughtful, realistic and much-needed advice for young adults but in a fun and lighthearted approach. It's a game-changer! This is a perfect, anytime gift, and I will be giving copies to the young men I work with.

—Daniel Alexander, Sigma Nu House Director, University of Tennessee

In *Adulting 101*, Pete and Josh have compiled a key resource for you as an early twentysomething beginning your life journey. Keep this book handy to see what you should be considering as you make life decisions.

—Russ Crosson, author and Chief Mission Officer for Ronald Blue Trust

I have received life-changing guidance and wisdom from Pete for the last twenty years. I can't think of a more qualified person to write this book. *Adulting 101* will help you accomplish your goals and be the person you've always wanted to be. If you are nearing graduation or are on your own for the first time, read this ASAP.

—Steve Canter, college football coach and performance consultant,
The CanterZone LLC

Sometimes life lessons come the hard way. *Adulting 101* smooths the rough road and will spare young people (and the people who mentor young people) headaches that can easily be avoided.

—Sean McGever, Professor, College of Theology at Grand Canyon University

Adulting 101 is for anyone who has said, "Nobody told me that!" I find myself using this insightful book as a home base for my life strategy.

—Will Jarrett, recent college graduate

Adulting 101 should be a required textbook in our schools and homes! This resource could be a game-changer for parents who want to come alongside their children and truly prepare them for a successful adult life.

—Reverend Brandon Watson, Minister to Young Adults,
Immanuel Baptist Church, Little Rock, AR

Adulting 101 will serve for many as a safe place to discover that they are not alone in their struggles to discover the secrets of independence in this new season of life.

—Chris Lawson, Chief Creative Officer, Everyday Exiles

Adulting 101 is a terrific resource to give you practical tools, so that you can live your life in such a way that it leaves a distinguishing mark for all of eternity.

—Mark Henry, Teaching Pastor, Fellowship Bible Church, Little Rock, AR

Empowering, encouraging, and enlightening—this book is a game-changer!

—Jody Jean Dreyer, thirty-year Disney veteran and
author of *Beyond the Castle: A Guide to Discovering Your Happily Ever After*

Adulting 101 highlights key lessons for evolving into adulthood. The tips and tricks emphasized in the book aren't taught in schools, and they will help to prepare you for real-world experiences.

—Sidney Webb, student, University of Arkansas

This book is packed with valuable advice that will help you navigate the open waters of adulthood where most of the obstacles are hidden from view. Consider *Adulting 101* your map.

—Ben Arment, author of *Dream Year*

Pete is the most qualified person I know to write this book. I'm so excited to add *Adulting 101* to my resource library.

—Peter Eberly, Church Planter/Lead Pastor, Eastside Church, Harrisonburg, VA

Adulting 101 is a must-read for young people. It's full of all the things you wish they would teach in school, but they rarely do. It's real, relatable, and easy to read all while giving students the edge they need to be successful in life.

—Amanda Jaeger, news anchor, Miss Kansas America 2014

As a graduate with a yearning to wring out every ounce of life, this book is exactly the tool I needed.

—Bryson Wong, recent college graduate

This book is an excellent starting point to outline the basics of what financial understanding and responsibility as an adult looks like.

—Austin Bryan, CFP®, Financial Adviser

I've heard wisdom defined as "being skillful in the art of living." For over twenty-five years, I've known Pete Hardesty and seen him demonstrate great wisdom time and time again. He has helped countless high school and college students successfully make the transition from adolescence to adulthood. *Adulting 101* is full of practical wisdom and will be a great resource for any young adult.

—Danny O'Brien, founder and CEO, Avila Home Care

Adulting 101 equips and enables the reader with the tools they need in their transition into adulthood. In addition, it serves as a great reminder for those of us who are already there (or who think we are) to never stop in the learning process.

—Matt Summitt, investment banker

ADULTING 101

101

#WISDOM4LIFE

JOSH BURNETTE
&
PETE HARDESTY

BroadStreet
PUBLISHING

BroadStreet Publishing® Group, LLC
Savage, Minnesota, USA
BroadStreetPublishing.com

ADULTING 101: #WISDOMFORLIFE

978-1-4245-5636-6 (hardcover)
978-1-4245-5637-3 (e-book)

Disclaimer: The purpose of this book is to provide helpful information
around the areas discussed. The authors and publisher recommend you seek
professional help as needed and cannot take personal responsibility for how the
reader applies the information and its ultimate results.

Stock or custom editions of BroadStreet Publishing titles may be purchased in
bulk for educational, business, ministry, fundraising, or sales promotional use.
For information, please email info@broadstreetpublishing.com.

Cover by Chris Garborg at garborgdesign.com
Interior by Katherine Lloyd at theDESKonline.com

Printed in China
18 19 20 21 22 5 4 3 2

CONTENTS

YOU CAN CHANGE THE WORLD

"**I** don't know what goes where. I've never filled out a check before."

I thought the college sophomore was kidding with me. But he wasn't. He was paying for an overnight excursion trip we were going on with about one hundred and fifty students, and he didn't know how to write the check to pay for it.

"Can you tell me which address goes where?" A junior asked me this question as we were writing thank-you notes to people who had helped with a fundraiser. Again, I thought he was kidding. Nope. He didn't know where to write the recipient's address or the return address on a piece of mail.

That was when I realized that most of the students I worked with were not prepared for real life. They had studied in school for twelve grades (thirteen including kindergarten) and then four-plus years in college, yet after those sixteen-plus years, they were still lacking some of the basic adult "survival skills."

And although the checkbook and postal problems mentioned above are fairly easy to remedy (we can Google how to do just about anything these days), having some real-life survival skills can keep young people from literally ruining their lives.

I know someone who racked up tens of thousands of dollars in credit card debt (starting after high school with the purchase of a big-screen TV) because he never acquired financial survival skills. Both he and his wife are now working two jobs to pay for mistakes he made years ago.

But I'm going to make a difference in this world, you're probably thinking. *And my credit card balance isn't that high.*

We also believe you're here on this earth to be a world-changer. You matter, and your life has an incredible purpose. So part of this next stage of the journey as a "new adult" is to find out what matters to you—spiritually, emotionally, physically, and relationally—and how you will give yourself to these things.

Most people want to make a difference. If you don't, you can just stop reading right here. This book is meant for people who want to leave this world a better kind of different than they found it.

But you probably also need a job, a place to live, and a budget.

Oh, man, you sound like my parents.

And you've probably got questions about dating, relationships, and marriage.

Okay, you really do sound like them. Stop.

We're going to try to not sound like parents, and instead sound like two guys who have also been trying to be world-changers as we've become adults. We've learned a ton from our mistakes, as well as from wisdom we've sought out and that's graciously been given to us along the way. As you seek to make your mark on this world, we want you to thrive, not just survive.

HOW TO CHANGE THE WORLD

James Hunter, in his volume *To Change the World*, suggests that change happens from the top down. We would like to suggest it also happens from the inside out.

How do you change the world? It starts with … *drumroll, please* … you. You're not in control of the world, but you are in control of yourself—how you think, feel, and behave.

Think of this book as a greenhouse. What happens in a greenhouse? Growth. How? The conditions in the greenhouse are set for optimal growth. What we will talk about for the rest of the book is how to set the conditions of your life (that you are in control of) for growth.

Growth doesn't just happen. It involves hard work, effort, and intentionality. What is your personal growth plan? Do you have one? (See chapter 18.) How will you get better? Zig Ziglar, a famous American author and speaker, would say, "If you aim at nothing, you'll hit it every time."[1]

This book is designed to be a practical guide to a life well lived. We hope to help you chart a course for your life from the fifty-thousand-foot view, but also help you right down on the runway.

In this book, you will be equipped with:

- An exercise on how to discern your mission in life and give your life to what matters
- Tips and tricks on how to be wildly successful at work
- A step-by-step guide to your finances so you can become a millionaire (yes, we said millionaire)
- Goal-setting and time-management skills so you can spend more time doing what you love and less time doing what you hate
- Simple, easy-to-understand counsel on complicated topics such as insurance, credit, purchasing cars and homes, and more
- Research on how to do well in the first few months in college or after graduation
- Instruction for building better relationships with those around you and caring for people in a deeper way
- And much more

This book is about surveying your life for the long term but also practically helping you with the day-to-day. It's about how to have impact, how to live a life of excellence and legacy, and how to get the most out of life. You want the life of the person you admire, but they paid a price for the life they have lived. They sacrificed, worked hard, took chances, grinded it out, and continued to press on through hard circumstances. And they were rewarded.

You're at the beginning of your journey. You have vast adventures that lie ahead.

You want to be a world-changer.

You were meant to be a world-changer.

Let's release you to be a world-changer.

1

#THEHEARSEANDTHEUHAUL

The phone rang. I (Pete) was the only one in the office so I answered it. A deep, gravelly man's voice said, "I need to speak with the person in charge of your chapter at Princess Anne High School."

Uh-oh. These calls could be trouble. I was on staff with a nonprofit organization that worked with high school students, and we never knew what to expect with these kinds of calls. Often, they were from parents worried about their kids.

"I'm the one in charge," I said. "How can I help?"

"We need to have a meeting," the bellowing voice said.

"Okay. May I ask what it will be in reference to?"

"I want to know how I can help you."

Phew. I felt like I had dodged a bullet, and the next week I met a man who would change my life forever. His name was Jack Birsch, and at the time, he was well over three hundred pounds, had a shiny bald head, and was smoking a big cigar. At noon. In a Holiday Inn restaurant (one of the few places left in Virginia Beach that allowed smoking). It was the beginning of a friendship that would change me forever.

We started meeting once every couple of weeks, then every week for an hour, and then every week for two hours. Jack had a twinkle in his eye and a way with words. He was big on grace. He was big on love. And he had a big personality.

After we had met several times, he asked me a question I would never forget. It would become a splinter in my mind. "Have you ever seen a hearse pulling a U-Haul?"

I thought about it. "No."

"Of course you haven't," he said. "Because naked you come and naked you go. So you better find out what matters in this life and give yourself to it wholeheartedly."

Jack asked me that question every few weeks until it became engrained on my heart. As I got to know him, I realized that the impact of his life was still echoing all over Virginia Beach and the world. It seemed like almost every day I would meet someone who would say, "Oh, Jack? He was a huge influence in my life. He showed up when I needed him most."

BEGIN WITH THE END RESULT IN MIND

Take a minute to think about your funeral. Pleasant, I know. But close your eyes and imagine what it would be like. Who will be there and what will they say? If you passed away tonight, how would you be remembered? Would people be sad or indifferent? Who would be there saying you made an impact on them? Have you made a difference in this world?

Unsettling, isn't it? Morbid? Sobering? Yes, it is. We all think we're going to live forever. But here's the reality: the death rate is holding steady at one per person. You will die. It's just a matter of when and how.

One of my mentors, Ralph (I called him Rev), had people from many countries come to his funeral. They traveled from all over the world to honor and pay their respects to someone who had impacted their life. Rev found out what mattered during his life.

We are temporary stewards of everything in our life. We are to responsibly manage what we have while we're here, but none of it goes with us when we die. This may seem disappointing at first, but really, it's good news. It is freeing. No possessions last forever, nor are they meant to. Dead people can't enjoy their stuff.

If we figure out what matters, we can have a life well lived. We can have an impact that lasts beyond us, maybe even forever. I'll give you a hint: What you have isn't what matters. Here's the reality: You matter. What you do matters. People matter. You were meant to make a difference in this world.

Stephen Covey says that we should begin with the end result in mind.

He lists this principle in his book *The 7 Habits of Highly Effective People*. Most people want to have a meaningful life—but most don't. Most people want to have a difference-making life—but most don't. Most people want to make a huge impact during their life—but most don't.

What are you going after? Who do you want to be? A meaningful life will not just happen. You can't achieve great things simply by binge-watching Netflix. No one ever drifts into greatness. No one ever drifts into making a difference. You need to be intentional. You have to live with a purpose.

What's important to you? If you don't quite know yet, that's okay. You're at a discovery stage of life and trying to find out what matters and what's important. Many things will try to coax you away from investing yourself in the important things. Some of them will even be "good" things. Some will seem urgent, but they won't really matter in the grand scheme of life and your existence. You must give yourself to the important. The vital. The things that matter.

There may be a sense of loss, sadness, or disappointment when you graduate (or when you graduated) because you always hear people talking about college as the "good old days." If this is true, then we're all in big trouble. That means the rest of your life is a depressing downward spiral—that you peaked when you were twenty-one? Not a chance. I can assure you that every season of life brings opportunities for more satisfaction, fulfillment, and joy. College is an incredible time of life and a special time, but the reality is: The best years are yet to come.

YOUR DEATHBED REGRETS

As you think about your funeral, as you begin with your end result in mind, what would you change? What regrets do you have? Have you ever been with someone when they were near death? It's a profound time when the divide between the temporal and the eternal becomes thin. When we're witnesses to the finality of life, we reflect and maybe even regret, but whatever truly matters to us crystalizes quickly. At the end of your life, what will stand the test of time?

Top 10 Life Regrets

Here's a (paraphrased) list of people's top ten regrets at the end of life, according to an addicted2success.com study of residents in nursing homes:

1. I wish I had lived a life true to myself, not the life others expected of me. I wish I hadn't compared myself to others.
2. I wish I hadn't worked so much and wish I'd made more time for my family.
3. I wish I'd had the courage to express my feelings more. I wish I'd allowed myself to love, be loved, and say I love you.
4. I wish I had stayed in touch with my friends.
5. I wish I had pursued my dreams and aspirations, persevered, and kept going. I wish I discovered my purpose earlier.
6. I wish I had saved more money for retirement.
7. I wish I had taken more risks and more chances/traveled more/experienced more cultures.
8. I wish I had realized contentment and happiness are a choice. It's all about your perspective and attitude.
9. I wish I had taken better care of myself—physically, emotionally, and spiritually.
10. I wish I had touched more lives and inspired more people.[1]

WHAT'S YOUR MISSION STATEMENT?

People with clearly defined missions have always led those who haven't any.
You are either living your mission, or you are living someone else's.
—Laurie Beth Jones, *The Path: Creating*
Your Mission Statement for Work and for Life

It was said that during World War II, if an unidentified soldier appeared in the dark and could not state his mission, he was automatically shot.[2] Mission in World War II was a matter of life and death.

It still is. Your mission is the most important thing you can do with your life. What are your life values? Can you name three? Can you name one? What are your unifying principles (overarching guiding principles that help you stay on purpose)? Other factors that are vital to your mission are your strengths and passions. There are many tools to help you discern your strengths including StrengthsFinder and Enneagram, or search "best strengths finder test" for several free diagnostic exercises. What do you want to accomplish in this world?

You might not know and that's okay. But the sooner you discover your purpose and figure out your mission, the sooner you'll be able to accomplish it. The sooner you will have a lens through which to make decisions. Here are some questions to meditate on to craft your personal mission statement:

- If you could change one thing in the world, what would it be?
- If you could influence a cause, what would you choose?
- What are some issues that you're passionate about?

RAGING RIVERS

In grad school, I had a professor who was recognized as the world's authority on his teaching topic. He had a PhD from Yale and a PhD from Harvard, and his textbook was the gold standard. One of the students in my class asked, "Prof, how do you keep learning? Haven't you arrived?"

He slowly walked closer to us and kept silent for what seemed like minutes. Then he replied, "That's a good question and a foundational one. As soon as you think you've arrived, it's the beginning of the end. I always want my students drinking from a raging river and never a stagnant stream."

So how do you have a life well lived? How do you avoid those top ten regrets?

You start today. You put the big rocks in first (more on this in chapter 17). You do the first right thing each day. You find your purpose and your mission and what gives meaning to life. If you want to make a difference, you're going to have to take risks.

Let's embark on this adventure together. Here's to becoming raging rivers.

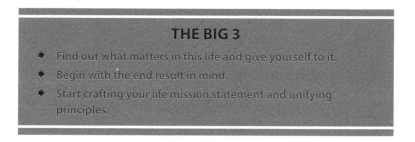

THE BIG 3

◆ Find out what matters in this life and give yourself to it.

◆ Begin with the end result in mind.

◆ Start crafting your life mission statement and unifying principles.

#LEAVINGAWAKE

If you've ever ridden on a boat and turned around, you've seen that the water was disrupted and came out differently behind the boat. This disruption of water is called a wake. Each of us leaves behind a wake as we go through our lives. Some of those disruptions are good and others are bad. After I (Josh) met Pete, my life looked completely different than it did before—in a positive way. His wake leaves people different.

My good friend Josh Goodman is the same way. He's one of the coolest guys I've ever met. After freshman year, he asked me to be his roommate (I'm still not sure if he just felt sorry for me). For the next three years we lived in a house with some other guys, and I never dreamed how that would change me for the rest of my life.

Each off-campus student house at James Madison University (JMU) has a nickname, and I moved into the one called the Treehaus. It consisted of eight of the most insane, life-loving, intentional men who have ever been placed on the earth, and I learned so much from them, but especially from Josh—or Goody, as we call him.

LIVING THE GOOD-Y LIFE

Goody is the kind of guy who knows everyone. And I mean everyone. JMU had nearly twenty thousand people on campus, and Goody won "Mr. JMU" in his freshman year. We would walk into a dining hall, and it would take us ten minutes to get a table because so many people stopped him to say hi. It was like living with a local celebrity.

Goody was (and still is) also one of the busiest people I've ever met. He played every intramural sport, volunteered for the same nonprofit as me, went to every professor's office hours, had awesome grades, and was just an all-around rock star.

Yet despite everything he had going on, he always had time for me. He would stop me and ask a deep question that went way beyond how class was going, teaching me the value of intentional questions. But he didn't just ask questions. He listened to my answers. And then he asked questions based on what I answered. He didn't come preloaded with what he wanted to communicate or anxious for me to finish talking so he could tell me about himself. Goody taught me what it looked like to ask questions that dug far below the surface and how to genuinely know someone.

My wife and children have a different husband and father because of the guys I lived with during college, especially Goody.

WHAT'S YOUR WAKE LIKE?

There's no doubt that Goody, like Pete, left a positive wake in my life. What kind of wake do you leave? You will leave one regardless of whether you intend to or not. Pete is intentional about leaving people in a better place after their interactions with him. Today you will interact with dozens or maybe even hundreds of different people. Will they be better people after interacting with you?

How do you leave a positive wake? First of all, remember that you're influencing people whether you want to or not. Therefore, if you want to positively affect someone's life, you need to be intentional about it. Instead of waiting for someone to call you or invite you for coffee, seek them out. After reading this chapter, contact someone you want to positively influence and get together with them. You'll need to be face-to-face and hear their voice to have a meaningful interaction. Very few strong, intentional relationships are built on texting.

Second, be genuine. People know fake, and if you pretend to care about someone, it will have the exact opposite effect of what you originally intended. An example of this is the classic question of "How are you doing?" People ask this all the time. You probably asked and were asked this question several times today. If we're honest, most people don't really care; it's just what you're supposed to say when you see someone. You're quickly saying hello, then moving on with your day. But if you stop, look someone in the eye, and say, "How are you really doing today?" that can alter the entire dynamic of the relationship. That simple question can tear down walls and even change lives.

Third, ask more great questions. This is a lost art form. Often, we are tempted to keep questions strictly on the surface level, even with our closest friends. Dive a little deeper. Ask people "Why?" more often and continue to peel back the layers behind their original answer.

Don't just talk about what you did that day. Learn about who they are, how they think, and how they process information. Don't just ask about an event. Inquire how they felt as a result. What are they learning? Have they read a great book recently, and what did they learn from it? Ask others what they believe about religion and politics and then listen to them without trying to change their minds. It is easy to ask simple questions that don't give you a full understanding of someone; this is the danger of a texting or snapping relationship. It's not a very deep or personal relationship.

Last, you need to be available. No one leaves behind a long-term positive impact because they were too busy for others in their life. One of Pete's mentors, Chuck Reinhold, would always ask, "Are you a 'Here I am!' or a 'There you are!' type of person?" It's difficult to change the world being a "Here I am!" person. The more you learn the reality that "it's not about you" the more impact you will have. And the more fulfilled you will be. Be others-centered and seek to understand before seeking to be understood (another habit highlighted in Covey's *The 7 Habits of Highly Effective People*).

Perhaps you've read through this chapter and are thinking, *I wish I had a mentor like Pete to teach me.* I encourage you to first look at yourself and see if you're ready for a mentor like this. It doesn't just happen. Find someone who is a little older than you that you want to be like in some way. Get coffee with them and ask them questions. Learn how they became successful. If they are happily married, ask them to share marital wisdom with you. No one is going to just walk up to you and ask to be your mentor. You have to seek someone out. And don't just say, "Will you mentor me?" That is a huge responsibility and can scare people off. Just begin with a coffee or meal to learn more about the person. Find people that are willing to pour into you and learn as much as you can from them.

Now that you have someone sharing wisdom with you, you need to pass it on. Guess what? You are already that older and wiser person that people look up to. Have you made yourself available and been intentional with them? Have you gone out of your way to care for and engage with people? Regardless of your age, if you're reading this book, there are people younger than you who want to spend time with you and learn from you. You have the opportunity to leave a huge positive wake in their life—to be a Pete or a Goody to those around you. Don't underestimate your impact.

THE BIG 3

+ Never underestimate the impact you have (you may never know its full effect).
+ Be intentional, genuine, and available.
+ Ask awesome questions.

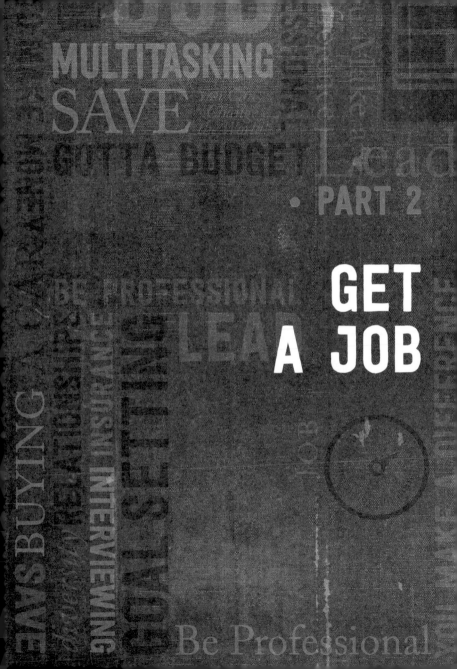

PART 2

GET
A JOB

3

#PURPLEHAIRINTERVIEW

*Adults are always asking kids what they want to be
when they grow up because they are looking for ideas.*
—Paula Poundstone, comedian

It was March 2012 and I (Josh) had recently become the Owner/ Operator of one of the poorest-performing Chick-fil-A restaurants in the country. I needed new employees—badly. We were understaffed and the team we had was underwhelming. (Most of us have been to a restaurant where you seemed to be an inconvenience to the people who were there to "serve" you. It makes you never want to come back.) As a new business owner, this was terrifying to me. I needed to hire a new team to transform our poor customer service.

I had a brilliant idea: What about open interviews? We decided to hold the interviews at a set time each week so there were no surprises for candidates interested in a job. It gave them the opportunity to prepare and look professional for the interview and perhaps even bring a résumé.

Our first scheduled time for open interviews was a disappointment. *Disappointment* isn't even the right word. *Catastrophe* better described this round of interviews. I'll never forget the group of people waiting for me to come out and interview them for a job.

One young woman I interviewed first had purple hair. Not a small section of hair, but her entire head. All right, purple hair can be fixed, but then I realized what she was wearing (or rather, wasn't wearing). Her top was completely sheer. Essentially, she was interviewing in her bra and ripped jeans. She filled out the application in sparkling pink ink. Part of her email address was crazywoman1.

FIRST IMPRESSIONS AREN'T FAIR

Does this young woman seem like the type of person who would represent me, my restaurant, and my company well? Definitely not, based on first impressions alone. I realize that she could have been the sweetest person in the world and that she probably just wanted to look unique. However, in a work environment where you have to serve customers and be the face of an organization, it's essential to present yourself professionally.

You will be evaluated immediately upon entering a room for an interview. You will even be assessed prior to the interview based on how you fill out your application. Many employers even look at your social media accounts, so be sure to check your public online presence and confirm that it will be presentable to a business looking to hire you.

ATTRACTING THE RIGHT KIND OF ATTENTION

Applying for a job is similar to getting a person to date you. Every interaction is an impression in their mind. Think about what you do when you find someone who you're attracted to and want to get their attention. The first interaction with a potential employer is like a first date. You want to do so well on that first date that you'll get a second date (or a job).

First, you would probably peruse social media to discover what they're interested in. You're going to do your research. Next, you'll want to begin tailoring your interests to theirs. Then, the next time you know you'd see this person, you'd be in your sharpest attire. You want to show the very best version of yourself.

Don't confuse this with not being yourself. You absolutely want to be who you are and not give a fake impression. But whether it's an interview or a date, make sure you're aware of how you look and behave, and the general impression that you're giving.

So, if you've been able to land an interview (first date) with a potential employer, here's how to prepare:

1. Get background information about the company. Know what they do and why they do it. Learn about the history of the organization. Create a couple of intelligent questions as a result of your research. Make sure you want to be connected to this organization. Do your values align? Are you excited about what they're trying to accomplish in the world? This shows you care about their mission and that you're willing to spend forty (or more) hours each week working toward that mission.

2. Speak to your references. Let them know about the upcoming interview and to expect a call or email from someone. Make sure you've selected great references and not family members or friends (you're immediately discounted if your references are your mom, friend, or brother). Instead, include previous bosses, pastors, coaches, mentors, teachers, or principals as your references; these people will give a more objective assessment of your qualities.

3. Call the day prior to confirm the scheduled appointment time.

4. Have someone mock interview you. Role play. Have a friend who has a job ask you possible questions so your first time answering questions isn't in front of your potential boss. Have them ask about your greatest strengths, areas you need to work on, what you're passionate about, etc. This is more about being comfortable answering questions than giving a perfect response to the mock interviewer.

5. Have a professional email account for your application and résumé. Spoiledprincess95 or 1toughguy are not appropriate for the business world. Create an account (many people use Gmail) that is your first and last name. Add your middle initial or some distinguishing number if you need to.

Once you're feeling comfortable with the time leading up to the interview and have prepped well, you're ready for the big day. And remember, it's a conversation and not a presentation. If you go into it worried about me, me, me, then you'll be wound up too tight. Be sure to breathe.

HOW TO HAVE AN AWESOME INTERVIEW

1. Dress professionally. Don't wear a T-shirt or jeans, sheer material, anything with a stain or hole in it, or anything that will expose your underwear. Wear a suit if you're a man, and professional blouse, slacks or a skirt, and a blazer if you're a woman. It doesn't matter if you're interviewing for a fast-food job or an accounting job; you need to dress above the position you are applying for. That makes an indelible mark on the mind of the interviewer.

2. Show up early. Nothing is less impressive than a candidate who barely makes their way through the door when the interview is supposed to start. This is the quickest way to not get hired. If you can't be on time when you desperately want a position, there's no way you'll ever be on time when you actually have the job. Showing up early communicates professionalism and preparation.

3. Shake hands with your interviewers, and do it like your handshake will dictate your ability to get the job. This shows strength.

4. Throughout the interview, be sure to maintain eye contact. Not in a creepy way, but it seems like you're hiding something when you don't make eye contact. Practice with a friend beforehand. Stare at them for thirty seconds so it doesn't feel awkward during the interview.

5. Smile during the interview. A smile is the easiest way to break down barriers, whether it's with an interviewer, a customer, or even a family member.

6. Speak with enthusiasm. Nothing is harder for an interviewer to listen to for thirty minutes than a monotone robot. Change the inflection of your voice. Show passion behind your answers. Don't scream at the interviewer, but make sure they know you have a pulse.

7. Many employers will ask you situational questions such as "Tell me about a time when …" They want to see that you have experienced different situations and can think of a response on your

feet. You should have three or four stories that are versatile and can be used in several different responses to showcase your abilities. This will allow you to pivot in case you can't think of a specific example of what they're asking for. Demonstrating confidence is more important than getting it exactly right.

8. They will want to hear about your story. "Tell me about yourself" needs to be responded to with brevity and substance. Don't ramble about when you were born, what your childhood was like, middle school, etc. That doesn't matter. Talk about where you're from, what you love to do, your future goals, and experiences that would relate to what they're looking for in the position you're applying for.

9. Your interviewers will want to know about your future. Have some clearly defined goals (we will touch on this later in the book). This shows intentionality and purpose. You're not just applying to this job haphazardly; it plays a critical role in the skills you want to develop to move forward.

10. Often, you will be asked about problem-solving skills. Have an example in mind prior to arrival. Think through a time that was challenging, what actions you took to solve the problem, and what that resolution was.

11. You may be asked about strengths and weaknesses. It is always easier to give your strengths than your weaknesses. When discussing your weaknesses, don't give masked strengths (you sound silly doing this). "Caring too much" is not a weakness, nor is it true. Give them an honest weakness as well as what you're doing to combat it.

12. If you're asked about hobbies or interests, don't say "hanging out with friends." Everyone hangs out with friends. That is not a worthwhile skill that communicates anything to the interviewer. Talk about your love of reading and the most recent book you've read. Speak about the sports team that you've been on for

several years. Tell them about the nonprofit organization you've been volunteering with. Let the interviewer see you giving your time to your community, a soup kitchen, a mentoring organization, etc.

13. Don't give short answers. This is the only time you have a chance to present yourself to this company. Give them depth without rambling. Make sure you fully answer each question without providing unnecessary details, and always give an example.

14. Ask great questions. Whether it's from your research or from asking questions about your interviewers' perspective on the company, you want them to know that you have the ability to ask insightful questions.

15. Clarify the next steps. Ask what their timeline is for selecting the candidate for the position. When can you expect to hear from them?

Whew! All done. You have prepared well and have wrapped up your interview. I hope you feel a weight off your shoulders. There is one final tip I could give you to set you apart from the rest of the field: Write a handwritten letter to each interviewer and sincerely thank them for their time. Don't send an email. I guarantee that your interviewers receive a lot of email each day. They don't want an email from you. A handwritten letter is an art. Write them a letter saying thank you. That will speak volumes about your professionalism.

YOU'RE HIRED!

Recently I conducted another interview, one very different from my interaction with crazywoman1. A young man named Tanner came into the restaurant in a suit and tie to pick up his application. You read that correctly. He was simply picking up the application, but he knew that every interaction is an interview, and he was prepared. He filled out his application, and we called him back for an interview.

He came to the interview in his suit and tie, and this time brought a résumé with him. He was only fifteen and had a résumé prepared. Clearly, he set himself above the rest of the candidate pool by coming prepared. He was nearly guaranteed the job before he even began answering questions. Throughout the interview process, he was incredibly polite, saying, "Yes, ma'am" and "No, sir." He gave articulate and thoughtful responses to each question, but Tanner blew away the competition before even opening his mouth. My team and I were impressed, and we hired him.

Disclaimer: I do want to warn you that even if you do everything in this list and feel as though you crushed the interview, that doesn't mean you'll get the job. You won't get every job you apply for, and that's all right. It's just a part of life. You're not a failure if you don't get the first job you apply for. Being turned down is a life lesson that is even more important than getting the job. Coping with "failure" is more important than celebrating success. If you feel as though you did everything and didn't get what you think you deserved, take heart. Keep plugging away. Most of the time, success results from persistence.

THE BIG 3

- Look the part. Always dress above what you should for the job.
- Be prepared with questions, a resume, and references.
- Practice, practice, practice.

4

#BEPROFESSIONAL

"**D**o you mean next Sunday cuz this Sunday has pasted already?"

The line above was an email I (Josh) received one Thursday afternoon. It was written by a young employee named Landon in regard to an event that was coming up that weekend for my restaurant. That was the entire email. No subject, no greeting, nothing. I saved it as an example to other young team members as how to not address your boss or any other person at your job—ever.

It's heartbreaking to see someone who has no clue how to engage with supervisors or even their peers. I've witnessed many of these young people come through my organization with little to no professional skills. Learning just a few basics will help propel you past your fellow teammates and set you up for success not only in the professional world but also personally. Let's dive into some of these skills to prepare you for success. We'll start by helping Landon out.

So why is Landon's email not correct? What's wrong with it? First, the entire email is set in a tone that communicates a lack of respect. It appears that he's just texting his buddy. Within the email there are many issues including:

- No subject line
- No greeting
- Incorrect spelling
- No punctuation
- No signature

Engaging with professionals requires a different kind of tone than texting your friend. It needs to communicate purpose and respect.

Here is how this email could have looked from Landon:

> Dear Josh,
>
> This is Landon, and I had a question about the restaurant event that you referenced in your email. Could you please clarify the date that the event will be occurring on?
>
> Sincerely,
>
> Landon

Now let's dive further into how to write a professional email and some helpful tricks to avoid costly errors.

EMAIL DO'S AND DON'TS

1. Have a professional-sounding email account. We addressed this in the interviewing chapter, but I can't put enough emphasis on the fact you don't want to email anyone with your middle school email account. Get an email that is your first and last name.

2. Never put the recipient into the *To* field until the very end. This may seem counterintuitive, but this little trick will save you from sending incomplete messages. Nothing is more frustrating than accidentally sending half of a message.

3. Have a subject line that communicates the purpose of the message briefly. Don't write *Hi!!!!!!!!!!* or *I have a question*. A proper subject line could be *Follow Up from Meeting with New Client* or *Leadership Meeting Notes on 7/12*.

4. Use the recipient's name at the start of the email.

5. Write out the content of the message in a concise manner. This is critical to the efficiency of your company, and it shows your recipient that you respect his or her time. Don't unnecessarily belabor a point.

6. Conclude with a professional signature (your name, title within the organization, contact information, etc.).

7. Read your email out loud before sending it.

8. Check all attachments. It would be unfortunate to send your boss

that weird picture of you with your cat as the attachment instead of the report you meant to send. Take the extra five seconds and double-check your attachments.

9. When setting up a meeting with someone, always include your availability. That will prevent unnecessary communications from going back and forth.

COMMUNICATION IS KEY

A huge part of being in any organization is responding to communications. This is an essential skill to develop while in the workforce. Whether the communication is sent via email, text message, smoke signal, or carrier pigeon, it is critical to show that you have received it, even if you can't send a full reply immediately.

The expectation in the workplace is that a phone call or email be followed up within twenty-four hours. For a text message, it should be within a few hours. Not all phone calls need to be returned. The only phone calls necessary to return are the ones that leave a message. If someone doesn't leave a message, then it generally communicates that they don't need a call back. And if you're leaving a voicemail, be sure to include who you are and why you're calling. This allows the person to know the context of the phone call and respond appropriately.

Speaking of voicemails, it's crucial to have your voicemail box set up. There is nothing more frustrating than listening to a phone go to voicemail, only to be greeted with the line, "The number that you are trying to reach does not have a voicemail box that has been set up yet. Good-bye." Or even better, "The mailbox is full at this time and cannot accept any messages. Good-bye." How many messages does it take to fill up a voice mailbox? Seriously. Listen to your messages, respond to them, and delete them.

The voicemail greeting on your phone should state your name, your company, that you're sorry that you missed the call, and that you'll get back to the individual as quickly as possible. Don't use a joke voicemail message, and don't use the default recording for the phone number.

Have something personalized so that when someone leaves a message, they know it is going to the proper person.

MY TIME IS MORE IMPORTANT THAN YOUR TIME

Communication is an important skill, but we can't continue talking about professionalism without addressing punctuality. Showing up to work promptly is the most critical of any of the topics that will be discussed. When you're expected to be at work at eight a.m., you never want to arrive at eight a.m. Arriving on time means you're late. Arriving five minutes before eight a.m. will communicate that you're on time, and arriving fifteen minutes beforehand will tell your coworkers and boss that you're early. Those fifteen minutes make an incredible difference in the way others perceive you. Are you the person sliding in at the final moment or the one who is ready and prepared to begin work at the appropriate time? Guess who will likely get promoted?

When you're late, you're communicating to other people that your time is more important than their time. It clearly states that the only person you care about is yourself. You're being selfish whether you realize it or not.

I learned this lesson the hard way while in college. At the time, I volunteered for a nonprofit, and every Friday we had a required leadership meeting that started promptly at five p.m. As you probably know, college guys aren't always the most punctual, and we'd made a habit of being late to this meeting. We showed up at 5:07, and our boss was mad. This night was the final straw.

In my mind, being late wasn't a big deal. I treated it like it didn't matter. But it did. When we walked in, about one hundred college students were seated and listening intently as my five friends and I headed toward any open seats. Naturally, none of those were in the back of the room. They were all perfectly positioned at the front of the room.

Our boss stopped the meeting and stared at us. He told us that when we arrive late we communicate to everyone else that our time is more important than their time. It is a piece of wisdom I've never forgotten.

At the time, being a few minutes late seemed harmless and not a big deal. But being rebuked by someone I greatly respected shifted how I thought about time for the rest of my life.

ALWAYS DRESS FOR SUCCESS— EVEN AFTER YOU'VE LANDED THE JOB

Now that you've arrived to work on time (early), it's essential to dress appropriately for not only the job that you have, but the job you want. If you don't dress to impress, then it will likely take you much longer to be recognized. Always dress one level above the expectation for your role. If you work in a casual environment, then dress snappy casual. If you work in a business casual environment, then wearing business attire will set you apart.

DON'T KILL THE MEETING

Throughout your career, you'll be involved in hundreds if not thousands of meetings. There is a certain etiquette associated with attending these meetings. Make sure you always come prepared. Confirm the topics in advance and prepare accordingly. Always get to the meeting five minutes before it begins; this communicates respect and allows the meeting to begin on time.

One person being late can cost a company lots of money in wasted time. Imagine that there are nine people in a room and all make twenty dollars an hour. They're waiting for the tenth member to arrive to begin the meeting, and that person shows up fifteen minutes late. Immediately, the company has lost forty-five dollars in productivity because just one person was late.

Always bring something to take notes with. You can't remember even 5 percent of what takes place during that time an hour later. Not taking notes clearly communicates that nothing said was worth remembering and therefore is a waste of time. Last, you need to walk away from each meeting with clear action items and due dates.

These basic skills will set you apart from those around you. Out of the gate, you'll be recognized as someone who is professional and has the capacity to take on more opportunities.

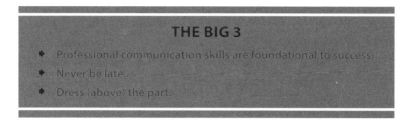

THE BIG 3

→ Professional communication skills are foundational to success.

→ Never be late.

→ Dress (above) the part.

#LEADORDIE

The task of leadership is not to put greatness into humanity,
but to elicit it, for the greatness is there already.
—John Buchan, author and politician

I have good news and bad news for you. Which do you want first?

Okay, here's the bad: Right now you want the job that you should have when you're thirty-three after working hard for ten years. Now the good: You want to make a difference in the world more than any other generation before you, and most of you are willing to grind it out. In this chapter, we'll show you that anyone willing to put in the effort can be successful at work and in leadership.

When I (Pete) moved to Harrisonburg, Virginia, to be the director of Young Life at James Madison University, the first meeting with all our volunteers was a complete disaster. Most were in college, and this was going to be the time for me to rally the troops, share the white-hot vision, and say, "Follow me!" If I could have ridden into the room riding a horse and carrying a sword, I would have. But they don't allow horses on campus, so after some mixers and some administrative business, I stood up. Every eye was on me. I had the movie *Braveheart* cued to the "Sons of Scotland" freedom speech for the perfect moment in my talk.

I told a quick story about being in Walmart the week before, unknowingly on the worst day of the year—college freshman move-in day! Complete with insanely long lines and insanely frustrated and emotional parents. As I continued to speak, I felt like I was going to cry. Not sure why. It wasn't an especially touching story, but at the end of it I started to cry. Three minutes into my "inspirational" talk. Not just a tear running down my cheek, but a full-out, ugly-sob cry. Can't catch your breath cry. Moaning. Weeping. All forty of our leaders were looking at me with wide eyes. I know they were thinking: *Who is this new leader? He's so unstable. He's weird. He cries about Walmart.*

After an uncomfortable time of sobbing, I squeaked out, "I don't have much to offer you, but everything I have, I will give you. Flowing through a broken life. I want to see you succeed." I had been overwhelmed by my move, starting a new job I felt unprepared and unqualified for, and exhausted. For whatever reason, this was the best thing that could have happened. People believed that I wanted them to succeed. Maybe they felt sorry for me. I learned some valuable lessons:

- In weakness, there is strength.
- In authenticity, there is strength.
- In humility, there is strength.

This began a journey that would be a wild ride. In the following years, we had tremendous growth in our organization and lots of changed lives in our community. It all began with brokenness, weakness, and humility. According to gold-medal winning U.S. Track and Field Olympian Wilma Rudolph, "Never underestimate the power of dreams and the influence of the human spirit. We are all the same in this notion. The potential for greatness lives within each of us."[1]

The most important thing you can do in leadership is to lead yourself. We've talked about this already. The second most important thing you can do in leadership is to develop other people. As Jack Welch, the former CEO of General Electric, said, "Before you are a leader, success is all about growing yourself. When you become a leader, success is all about growing others."[2]

> *IT'S NOT ABOUT YOU. The sooner you realize this, the better your life will be. The bigger an impact you will have. The more people you will influence. The more fulfilled you will be. IT'S NOT ABOUT YOU.*

Who are you dreaming for? Leadership is not just about employees or direct reports. Leadership is 360 degrees—you lead up, down, and all around. You lead your boss, your direct reports, and your peers. One of my mentors, Pat Goodman, always says, "We hold a crown above other people's heads and let them grow into it." What do you think about influencing others? It's the most important thing we can do on this earth. Here are some of the most important principles of leadership to help you along your journey.

20 PRINCIPLES OF LIFE-CHANGING LEADERSHIP

1. Lead yourself first. Develop the right habits and the right morning and evening "greenhouse routine." Grow. Read. Reflect. Meditate. Reserve frequent times of solitude and silence to recalibrate and make sure you are on the right path. As author John Maxwell says, "Leadership develops daily, not in a day."[3]

2. Get around people you want to emulate. Find several mentors who you trust and respect and who are successful in the things that you want to be successful in. Also take inventory of who is in your inner circle. Who are your closest friends? These people will determine your future. You will be like the five people you spend the most time with. So make them good!

3. You must serve in order to lead. Be humble. Genuinely care for people. Don't just serve your boss; serve your coworkers and even those you supervise.

4. Dream for the people you lead. Develop them and have a vision for who they could become. See things in them that they don't see themselves. People are the only true resource in this world— and the most important one.

5. Speak the truth in love. Define reality, but be kind with the timing and how you speak.

6. Be hungry. Really, really hungry. Be a raging river. Relentlessly pursue getting better. Never be satisfied but always be celebrat-

ing. Go after your work and your life in general with gusto. Move fast. A moving boat is much easier to steer.

7. What you lift up and celebrate will get reproduced. Pay attention to what you encourage. Thank people extravagantly for a job well done—publicly and privately.

8. Have a white-hot vision. Talk about it all the time. Begin with the end result in mind. You have to know what you're after or you'll just spin your wheels.

9. Listening/perception needs to be one of your greatest skills. Repeat back to people what you hear them say. Develop your emotional intelligence and self-awareness. You can't listen in a hurry.

10. Don't take yourself so seriously. Take your mission seriously, but yourself not so much.

11. Dream big. Try something of heroic proportions. Take a big swing at something. Boldness. Relentless bravery. Persistence and grit will accomplish what you want over time.

12. Ask the right questions. Asking the wrong ones will get you the wrong answers. For example, don't ask, "*Whom* should I marry?" Instead ask, "*Should* I get married?"

13. Use the Integrity Trinity. This is where talk, behavior, and belief intersect; it's the congruency of these three life components. Are your words, behaviors, and beliefs consistent? Your goal as a leader should be to make the intersection of these three things as big as possible. People won't follow leaders who lack integrity or character.[4]

14. Whatever you do, do it with excellence.

15. Ask the question "What's the wise thing to do?" often. You may act differently, but when you go in the opposite direction of wisdom, you should go slow and get some counsel from people you trust. Use decision criteria. Ask yourself, *Based on my past experience, in light of my current situation, and knowing my future hopes and dreams, is this right?*[5]

16. Get the right people on your team. People of high character, competence, and chemistry. If someone you supervise can do something 80 percent as well as you, delegate it to them. Do the things only you can do.

17. Celebrate. Life is too short not to appreciate accomplishment, personally and in your people. Build a culture of fun. Don't be afraid to celebrate small wins as well as large ones. Encourage people honestly and specifically.

18. Have unbridled optimism but also define reality as you hope. As Henry Ford said, "Whether you think you can or you think you can't—you're right."

19. Give feedback often and candidly, and also ask for it in a safe manner. Be a raving fan publicly and a thoughtful critic privately.

20. Teamwork makes the dream work. But it's tough for this to happen without a team or a dream. Multiplication of leaders should be your obsession. It's the ultimate influence and how to leave a legacy. According to an African proverb, "If you want to go fast, go alone. If you want to go far, go together."

HOW TO BE WILDLY, STUPIDLY SUCCESSFUL AT WORK

A couple years into my first job after college, I supervised two people. Both came highly recommended and interviewed well, but they were very different. Let's call the first one Chloe. Chloe was quiet, reserved, and worked better in smaller groups but was faithful and dependable. The second person we'll call Danny. Danny was charismatic, funny, and shined in crowds, but he was unreliable. Over the next couple of years, I saw an important leadership principle in action. To have real, long-term influence, people must be faithful. At first, Danny wowed the crowds of kids that we worked with. They loved him. Chloe was overshadowed. But as time wore on, Chloe had a much bigger impact as she faithfully walked with kids and their families through difficult times.

Speaker and author Brian Tracy says, "Become the kind of leader that people would follow voluntarily, even if you had no title or position."[6]

Are you committed to your mission for the long haul? Nowadays, people look at their job as a stepping stone. What's the exit strategy? What's the next best thing? It's okay to look to the future, but not at the expense of the present. Remember the bad news at the beginning of the chapter: Right now you want the job that you should have in ten years. But also remember, your first job is not your last job. Here's how to get that job.

TOP 12 WAYS TO BE SILLY SUCCESSFUL AT WORK (AND EVENTUALLY GET THE JOB YOU ALWAYS WANTED)

1. Ask your boss how you can help him or her specifically. Set your boss up for success and make their job easier.
2. Clarify with your boss the two or three most important things you can do in your job. And then do them excellently. Practice the art of essentialism. Become really good at a few things.
3. Work hard. I mean really hard. Persevere. Demonstrate grit.
4. Volunteer for difficult projects. When you have the chance to participate in a group effort, perform way beyond expectations. Let your boss know that you want to develop yourself and your skills, so you are open to going to any conferences or extra workshops that they suggest.
5. Serve the people around you. Genuinely help your coworkers and your boss. It's amazing what you can accomplish when you don't care who gets the credit.
6. Find out people's love languages. Check out the book *The Five Love Languages* by Gary Chapman. People need different things. Get to know your people, and care for them the way they prefer.
7. Bring out the best in people. Find out what they have to offer and what motivates them, then help them get it. Help people operate in their areas of strength.
8. Ask your boss and your direct reports (if you have any) how they like to receive feedback. Ask your boss, coworkers, and direct reports for feedback. What are your growth edges (areas

you can improve)? You want evaluations because you want to get better.

9. Organize meals and activities outside work. It's okay if no one shows up.

10. Write lots and lots of handwritten notes. Thank-you notes, appreciation notes, notes after meetings, etc. These are gold in our digital, electronic age. One time I was doing the introduction for a nationally known big-time leader. I spoke for five minutes. He spoke for thirty minutes. Later that week, he wrote me a handwritten thank-you for the introduction I gave him. Unbelievable! One of my friends, Brian, wrote a thank-you to a friend's dad for taking him out to dinner (with a big group). That dad ended up taking Brian on an all-expense-paid snowboarding trip to Lake Tahoe later that year, all because Brian wrote him a handwritten thank-you. But getting trips to somewhere exotic is not why we write thank-you notes. We write them because of what it communicates. It's not just the right thing to do; it's also the smart thing to do.

11. Encourage lavishly and offer extravagant appreciation for a job well done. Treat people with Starbucks or other things from time to time. Surprise them with thoughtfulness and kindness. It's contagious.

12. Value people and help them, especially when they can't pay you back or do you a favor. You will reap what you sow. It's one of the laws of the universe.

Think about the best boss you've ever had. Did they care about you? Of course they did. When your boss cares about you, you want to work harder. What else did they do that made them a good boss? My guess is they also cared deeply about the organization that you were a part of. If you want to really succeed at work, serve with integrity. Don't compromise. No job too big, no job too small. Look for greatness in the people around you, and bring it out. Do these things, and you will be silly successful at work.

According to an ancient Chinese proverb, "Watch your thoughts, they become your words. Watch your words, they become your actions. Watch your actions, they become your habits. Watch your habits, they become your character. Watch your character, it becomes your destiny."

The stakes are so high. If you don't lead yourself and others, destinies are up for grabs. There are unique things that you're supposed to do that only you can do. People you're supposed to impact. Causes you are meant to champion. Personal demons you are meant to battle and overcome. You. Must. Not. Shrink. Back.

You must lead.

THE BIG 3

- Leadership is influence. You must lead yourself first.
- Leadership is a skill that cannot be developed overnight but must be built over the long haul.
- True leadership is developing other people and helping them grow. Leaders develop leaders.

PART 3

RELATIONSHIPS

#CHEMISTRYCOMPETENCE

Do you know who has the largest influence on your day-to-day life while you're at work? If you think it's your boss, you'd be wrong. It's your coworkers and peers. And you know what? They will always be there. So if you're someone who really dislikes being around others, this will be a constant struggle. Getting to know your coworkers and working well with them are life skills that will be crucial to your long-term success.

EMOTIONAL INTELLIGENCE

One of the most critical concepts you can learn is emotional intelligence, which is defined as "the capacity to be aware of, control, and express one's emotions, and to handle interpersonal relationships judiciously and empathetically."[1] Basically, it's connecting with people. Having competency in a field is incredible, but without chemistry it won't get you very far.

Based on research, 90 percent of high-performers in the workplace have a high emotional quotient (EQ), which is a measurement of emotional intelligence. Consequently, 80 percent of low-performers had a low EQ. Your ability to recognize and understand others' emotions will shift your entire workplace dynamic.[2] But where do you go and what do you do to grow your emotional intelligence?

Thousands of articles are available online to help navigate and hone this skill. Below is a list Gordon Tredgold included in an *Inc.* article on the subject:

1. Listen twice as much as you talk.
2. Respond rather than react.

3. Put yourself in the other person's shoes.
4. Apologize directly if you are at fault.
5. Don't interrupt others or change the subject.
6. Be vulnerable.
7. Empathize with others.
8. Create a positive environment.
9. Ask, don't tell.
10. Praise more.[3]

Remember, people won't care how much you know until they know how much you care. If you just slow down and take the time to listen and connect with others, it will alter the way you engage with everyone in your life. Whether with a coworker, spouse, or friend, you'll begin to change your relationships by engaging better with people.

Self-Awareness

A huge element of growing your emotional intelligence is simply being self-aware. If you aren't aware of how others perceive you, then you'll never be able to change. Here are a few of the best ways to become self-aware:

- Ask others. Talk to your friends, spouse, coworkers, and family, and hear what they have to say. Let them be honest with you without fearing recourse or your being defensive.
- Take a personality test. There are tons of these. I (Josh) personally love the DISC behavioral assessment tool. Myers-Briggs is the classic and most iconic personality test.
- Write down what you care about, such as what you prioritize in life and what you plan around.

When it comes to supervising employees, I know firsthand how a lack of emotional intelligence can affect someone's success at work. One of the finest team members whom I ever employed was named Leslie. She could manage hiring at the restaurant, write the schedule, move quicker than anyone, and work every position in the place. We had a positive working relationship. But she had a problem. No one else liked working with her. Without even meaning to, she spoke to her coworkers as though she were smarter, and her tone was condescending.

I'm sure you can think of someone in your workplace, fraternity/ sorority, study group, or family who is like Leslie. She knew the right answer, but it was the way she communicated it that frustrated her peers. I sat down with her numerous times to try to coach her because she had such a high capacity. However, even though given plenty of time and opportunity, she couldn't change her actions and tone. Consequently, we had to part ways. Leslie was incredibly skillful, but her inability to connect with her peers was her downfall.

Serve to Lead

Let's contrast Leslie's story to that of Michael. Michael came to work at Chick-fil-A as a shy, homeschooled sixteen-year old. He had a great interview so we hired him. What we loved most about Michael was that he was a natural encourager. He cared for his peers in a way that has left a permanent impression on me and the team. He constantly looked for opportunities to serve others. When it came time for leadership promotions, Michael was on that list, but not because of his deep Chick-fil-A understanding or charismatic leadership abilities. He was promoted because everyone loved to be around Michael. This model of servant leadership is what elevated him into a formal leadership position. Michael is a humble team player, and as Timothy Keller has said, "humility is not thinking … less of myself, it is thinking of myself less."[4] That's Michael.

How to Show Emotional Intelligence at Work

- Build a friendship. Find out about what's happening outside work. Know the names of your coworkers' kids, siblings, and/ or parents. Find out what your coworkers like to do in their spare time, their favorite movie, etc. The questions you can ask are limitless.

- Serve. Look for small ways to serve. Bring in donuts. Get someone else a drink while you're up.
- Encourage. Everyone wants to be around an encourager. If you can hardwire yourself to genuinely encourage others, you'll draw people to you and be well-liked.
- Don't expect anything. Don't do any of this because of what you'll get out of the relationship one day. People can see right through this façade.
- Stay humble. You could be the very best person in your field, but if you're a jerk, no one will care. Stay humble but confident in your interactions with those around you.

COLLABORATION

Imagine the world without Google or the Beatles or airplanes or even worse ... Ben & Jerry's ice cream.[5] These are famous examples of two or more people coming together and creating something that has altered the world forever. The book you are reading is the result of something called collaboration. Collaboration is defined as "a purposeful relationship in which all parties strategically choose to cooperate in order to achieve shared or overlapping objectives."[6] It is most successful if you have strong emotional intelligence.

Collaboration is the current state of the workplace. Millennials are screaming for more collaboration than any other generation before. What exactly does this mean for you?

The ability to engage and work with your peers will be a more crucial skill than ever before. As the work place is becoming more integrated with a constant flow of ideas, feedback and shared systems you need to be prepared to interact with people who are completely different from you. They will have completely different ideas. And that is okay. The differences are your organization's strength. By leveraging the talents of more than one person or department, you have the ability to break down silos and use the genius from several people or parts of the business. Collaboration will often lead to a far greater result than going it alone.

DIVERSITY

Strength lies in differences, not similarities.
—Stephen Covey

The most diverse place that many will be each and every day is the work-place. Sadly, we spend much of our lives surrounded by people who act, look, and think the same way that we do. Your job provides a beautiful opportunity to learn about people, ideas, and cultures that you had never experienced before.

One of the restaurants that I had the opportunity to lead was in a downtown area and was predominantly African-American. This was one of the first times in my life that I entered a room as a minority. But you know what? It became some of my fondest memories.

Working with people who come from backgrounds different than yours can sometimes be difficult. Why? Because you naturally assume that you are right. But the other person in the conversation also believes that they are right. Maybe they are; maybe you are; but the only way to learn is to listen. Listen and respect one another.

If we live from a heart of having mutual respect, the world would look a whole lot different. So much of the racial discord would be alleviated. Engage in conversations with others assuming that they believe what they believe for a good reason.

Today, go to someone who looks, believes, or acts differently and say hello. Get to know this person. You never know. Some of the people you love the most can be the most different from you on the surface.

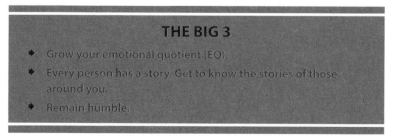

THE BIG 3

- Grow your emotional quotient (EQ).
- Every person has a story. Get to know the stories of those around you.
- Remain humble.

#ITSCOMPLICATED

The brain is an amazing organ. It works 24 hours a day,
365 days a year from birth until you fall in love.
—*Sophie Monroe*, Afflicted

It was my junior year of high school. I (Pete) had just gotten my license. A girl I had a crush on for a year was missing one day in band class. Her name was Isabella. She had long blonde hair, was from another country, and was a wonderful viola player.

I found out through some recon that she was sick. I thought, *This is my opportunity!* So I bought some flowers and chocolate and took them to her house. (Chocolate is exactly what you want when you're feeling sick, right?) We sat awkwardly for about an hour talking with her parents in the living room, and then she walked me out to the car. I told her I hoped she would feel better and gave her a hug. Our faces were close. I thought, *Oh my gosh, I'm going to kiss her*. (I also remember thinking, *I wonder if she's contagious?*) I might've even been puckering my lips with my eyes half closed.

But then she said, "Pete, I think you like me a lot more than I like you."

Ouch! I don't remember much after that. I think I stammered something like, "Oh no, I do this for all my friends," then jumped in my '86 Jetta and sped away with Bon Jovi's "Shot Through the Heart (You Give Love a Bad Name)" blaring through the stereo.

Relationships can be unbelievably confusing. They can lift us from despair to hope, from sadness to joy, from hurt to healing. They can lead us to new depths of friendship and even to the love of our life. They can be mind-bogglingly beautiful. But they can also leave us angry, crushed, frustrated, or spinning out of control. What can we do if our feelings overwhelm us? How do we make wise decisions so that our relationships become all they were meant to be?

WHAT IS THE PURPOSE OF DATING?

At your age and stage of life, what should your goals be? Finding a best friend and partner for life. Learning more about who you are. Having opportunities to serve and honor someone else.

If done right, dating can be for discovering who people are and getting to know them. Dating is as much about learning what you need and want and how you need to grow and change as it is about finding the "right" person. You can also learn a lot about yourself and some things that need to change. Dating is not just a means to an end. It's an opportunity to love, serve, honor, and have fun with someone. Take the pressure off. Learn relationship skills. Dating could become more than simply a way to find a mate; it could be a way to learn, grow, experience, and serve other people.

WHAT ABOUT DATING SOMEBODY FROM ANOTHER FAITH?

If you're a person of faith, you need to ask yourself this question about dating someone who has a faith-commitment different from yours. To answer it, you need to answer some other questions: *How serious am I about my faith? What role does it play in my life?* Because if your faith-commitment is a vital, deep part of you, how intimate are you hoping to get with your partner if, at the core of who that person is, he or she bases life on something else? This is along the same line as you and your partner not being on the same page about what you want to do regarding physical intimacy. Maybe you have certain standards, and he or she does not. Or after reading this chapter, you want to make a change, and he or she does not. If your partner doesn't care enough about you to honor you in this, he or she probably isn't the right person for you.

Your faith, taken seriously, is your foundation. If you and your significant other have different foundations, then anything you build will have a hard time standing. The basis for the entire relationship will be different, even divisive.

THE ANCHOR

In this wonderful and complicated world of relationships and love, we hear so many cultural voices that claim love is sex or sex is love. Or that sex is simply a physical act. Confused thinking leads to confused action. We want to provide clarity and wisdom around this complicated, exciting topic.

There is a type of love that seems to transcend this world. It's called *agape*. It is an others-centered love that has service at the core. It is the opposite of selfish. It doesn't change with circumstances. This chapter has agape love as its anchor. It's rooted in the idea of doing what is best for another.

Imagine what it would be like to have a friend who treats you this way, or to have a date that seeks *your* good first, not his or her own. Imagine what it would be like to become engaged to such a person and to marry with this kind of love at the center of your relationship. You would find yourself treated with kindness, devotion, and respect. You would be encouraged to become all you can be, to become your best self. And imagine if *you* cared for others this way; your life would be different. You would see others succeed and prosper. And this is the ironic secret to life—this is when we are most fulfilled. But this type of love is not cheap. It comes at significant cost.

Is sex good? *Yes!* It's actually more than good. It's great! When it is based in agape. When it is enjoyed under the right parameters within the confines of marriage.

In the movie *Spider-Man 2*, Peter Parker's Uncle Ben tells him, "You've been given a gift, Peter. With great power comes great responsibility."[1] God has given us all a gift—the gift of sexuality. This gift is the ultimate expression of intimacy and love. It's meant to be enjoyed, to be fun. It's powerful. It can even create new life. But the greater potential something has for good, the greater its potential for abuse outside its intended use.

Sex is like fire. Fire has incredible power for good. People can warm themselves by it, and fire gives light and enables one to cook. When it's utilized under the right parameters with the right boundaries, it can keep someone alive. But fire also has an incredibly destructive power.

Have you ever seen an out-of-control forest fire? A friend of mine saw his house burn to the ground. Everything he and his family owned was turned to ashes. If you asked him about fire at the time, he would've told you he hated it. It ruined his life.

Sex functions in the same way. It can be tremendous, but it can also be destructive when not enjoyed under the right circumstances. As sex experts Joe McIlhaney and Freda Bush say in their book *Hooked*, "When sex is experienced in healthy ways, it adds great value and satisfaction to life, but when experienced in unhealthy ways, at the wrong time, can damage vital aspects of who we are as human beings."[2]

A Word on Desire

Now, the desire for sex isn't wrong. In fact, it's very right. But this desire is designed to be fulfilled at a certain time and within certain conditions. When sex occurs outside of marriage, especially over and over again, it actually burns those who practice it.

Desire is innate. It's part of the package of our humanity. In and of itself, desire is good, not bad. But any good thing can be misused, even abused. In our view, the human problem around desire is not desire itself but *disordered* desire. We see this every day. For example, the desire to eat is great, and we need to eat—our bodies run on food. But gluttony is dangerous.

According to Pastor Tim Keller, "The human heart takes good things like a successful career, love, material possessions, even family, and turns them into ultimate things. Our hearts deify them as the center of our lives, because, we think, they can give us significance and security, safety and fulfillment, if we attain them."[3]

The desire for sex is a good desire. But we have misdirected it, bent and twisted it to something profane. Our culture elicits this appetite for sex from young people who don't have the maturity to handle it. Habitual behaviors are created that are destructive. Have you ever heard the end of any real-life story where sex was practiced outside its intended parameters? Most have common themes of brokenness, separation, guilt, pain, and regret. Few of us are willing to look at the truth and be honest with ourselves.[4]

Even Scientists Agree

Brain studies show that our behaviors shape physical neural pathways in our brain. It's like putting tracks down for future behaviors, good or bad, creating in us a tendency to do it again. When we have sex, it causes the release of dopamine, often called the pleasure hormone. Our brain then creates pathways that lead us to crave more sex. The more you do it, the more you crave it. The downside, however, is that the more you do it, the less it actually fulfills, without a long-term commitment to your partner. Your ability to bond and connect with someone is damaged if you have temporary sexual relationships.

When we take sex, which is meant for good, and use it poorly or badly, we hurt ourselves and those we have sex with. In *On the Meaning of Sex*, philosopher J. Budziszewski says: "Sexuality is like duct tape. The first time you use it, it sticks you to whomever it touches. But just like that duct tape, if you rip it off and then touch it to someone else, it isn't as sticky as it was before."[5]

Even "safe sex" won't change this result because there's no such thing as "safe" sex outside the marriage covenant. Taking precautions to not procreate children or contract sexually transmitted diseases doesn't lessen the power of sex. This is because sex is more than physical. It is spiritual and emotional as well. You are so much more than a physical being, and your sexuality is a deep part of who you are. While your identity is much deeper than your sexuality, your sexuality is still vital to your being.

A CLOSER LOOK AT RELATIONSHIPS, DATING, AND SEX

People have written entire books on these topics, and there are semester-long classes that just scratch the surface. For us to understand sex, dating, and relationships, we must first understand what they are not.

The Top Lies

1. *Lie: Sex is just not that big a deal. It's simply a physical act between two consenting people.* Everything you see, watch, and read from our culture will tell you that sex is just physical. Let me ask some questions that challenge this notion.
   + If sex is only physical, why is harassment and assault that is sexual more devastating and legally more serious than getting beat up by a bully?
   + If sex is "no big deal," why is our entire culture obsessed with it? Why is society consumed by it?
   + Why are some of people's biggest regrets sexual?
   + Answer to all of these questions: Because sex is more than physical. Sex is not just a body thing; it's a whole person thing. Neuroscientific evidence would support that sex cannot be separated from the whole person (despite the suggestions of our culture).

2. *Lie: Unconventional sex is normal and necessary to really be fulfilled.* Current cultural ideas of sexuality —as depicted on some wildly popular shows—are not correct. What just a few years ago was considered "deviant" has become commonplace, normal. Pornography has also distorted and ruined sex for countless numbers of people. Some have lived in a make-believe porn world for so long that the real thing doesn't match up anymore.

3. *Lie: God, if you believe in him, disapproves of sex.* The Bible talks about sex and sexuality, and there's a little on dating. But the Bible is clear that God invented sex. He's all for it and calls it good.[6] He is the author and authority on it. It is his design. If

you believe that God created sex, then you should realize that he knows best how sex is supposed to work and when. Marva Dawn writes in *Sexual Character* that "those who know the design of the machine are the ones most able to teach me how the machine can be most effectively used and maintained. The Designer knows the Design and is the best one to write the instruction book."[7]

4. *Lie: If you just find the right person, then everything will be all right. How do you know if you've found the right person? Chemistry.* Today, most couples don't build a relationship. Author Andy Stanley points out that when couples have a "chemistry" problem, most try to solve it physically and have more sex. For most men, sex is like a wrench—it fixes stuff. But people are in a relationship; they are not a chemistry equation. If you want to have a different marriage than others, you need to see beyond the chemistry you have with them. Are you treating yourself and those you date as if you are just a bundle of chemical reactions? You and your dates are much more than your bodies. In fact, chemically, it makes much more sense to wait till marriage to have sex. Did you know that the female brain releases oxytocin during intimate touching and sex? This is the "bonding" neurochemical, which is also released at the onset of labor and during breastfeeding to bond the mother to her child. But "oxytocin is values-neutral … it is an involuntary process that cannot distinguish between a one-night stand and a lifelong soul mate."[8] Males release vasopressin to bond/attach with their mates and their offspring. These two processes can contribute to feelings that linger post-breakup. Have you ever had sex with someone and then devastated when they start dating someone else, even though you don't want to be with him/her? Or have you witnessed couples where this is the case? Our chemistry can explain this. But you are more than your chemistry. You were designed to find your greatest earthly bonding experience through sex in a committed marriage, not in "casual" sex.

5. *Lie: Practice makes perfect. You should try to have sex as much and as often as you can.* Think for a second about your future spouse (if you get married). Would you want him or her to have had a lot of sex with a lot of people? If not, why not? Don't you want that special person to wait for you? Don't you think that person would want you to wait as well? Besides, all research points to better marriages among individuals who wait to have sex until marriage. Science shows that those who abstain from sex until marriage significantly add to their chances of avoiding problems and finding happiness. Every one of my friends who has waited until marriage to have sex with his wife has said he hasn't regretted it. Each one has said that sex has gotten better and better, not stale or boring as society would have us think. In other words, the best sex is marital sex, not casual, commitment-less sex.

6. *Lie: You should definitely have sex with someone you're considering marrying because you want to make sure that you "connect" on that level.* You would never buy a car without test-driving it, right? But there is no test-driving in the sexual arena. If you try to test-drive with someone, you'll be connected to that person. "Science shows that for young people to have the best chance of a happy life, they should wait until they are in a lifelong, committed relationship before having sex."[9] And that lifelong relationship is marriage.

7. *Lie: You were meant to be with one person, a soul mate. And your quest in life is to find that person.* Wrong. This is simply not true. According to Eric Metaxas, "The 'soul mate' idea suggests that marriage is all about *me*, that I need to find someone who understands *me* perfectly, who makes *me* happy. Marriage should be about finding someone *you* can make happy."[10]

8. *Lie: This part of your life isn't worth fighting for; it's not really worth all this effort and trouble.* On the contrary, a lifelong commitment to another person is so integral, so deep, so intimate, and so vulnerable that it is worth whatever it takes to do the right thing.

What do you want your life to look like in the future? One of the keys is thinking with the future in mind. You're not going to drift into victory in this area. You're not going to stumble into the right course of action. You're going to have to fight for it.

9. *Lie*: *You should decide who you're supposed to marry and let that guide your dating life.* We will get the answer to whatever question we ask, so we need to make sure that we ask the right questions. In this case, the correct question is *if*, not *who.* "Am I supposed to get married?" not "Who am I supposed to marry?" Marriage isn't for everyone, and neither is the single life. Which way you should go may not be clear to you yet. That's okay. There's no rush. And whatever you decide today doesn't have to be your forever decision.

10. *Lie*: *Each person gets one chance, and if you mess up, that's it. Attention: This might be the most important lie to hear the truth about.* If you think this, I have good news: No matter where you've been on this issue, you can reset where you're going. At any moment you can start over. You can begin to think differently about sex and make different choices. You are valuable and precious. You have dignity and worth. No one is beyond repair. No one is incapable of breaking the cycle. If you want to put a stake in the ground and say that from now on you will wait till marriage to have sex, it will be difficult. It will take courage. But it will be worth it. And it is necessary for you to become who you were meant to be. Scars can be made into beauty marks. This is not a message of condemnation but of hope and love.

Two Truths and a Lie

Truth #1: *"The present now will become your past, which will show up in your future"* (Andy Stanley).

We must make decisions with the future in mind. If you get married, your future spouse is probably dating someone this weekend who is not you. How do you want your future spouse to be treated? If you're dating someone, chances are (percentage-wise) you're not going to marry that person. How should you treat him or her? Use the golden rule when you're out on a date: treat the person you are dating the way you would want your future husband or wife to be treated.

Truth #2: *There are only two outcomes for dating relationships: getting married or breaking up.*

Can you date someone, not marry that person (break up), and have the entire process be a success? Yes, but it is tough. You should honor someone so much while you date him or her that if you break up, both of you would consider the whole experience a net positive. Kindness is honoring others with your treatment of them, but kindness is also honoring them by ending a dating relationship that needs to be ended.

The Lie: *Men and women are basically the same. They want the same thing, and see sex, dating, and relationships the same.*

Nothing could be further from the truth. So … many … differences! Not understanding the differences can be harmful to your dating health. Also, beware of how our culture presents sex. Isn't it odd that if a guy has a lot of sex with many different partners, he's labeled a stud, but if a girl has a lot of sex with many different partners, she's labeled promiscuous? Why is this? It's a double standard.

You are marvelously and wonderfully made. Your worth does not come from what you can do sexually; your worth is inherent. You have dignity in your humanity that no one can take away. The right person will honor this and see you for who you are, not what you can do in the bedroom.

There are emotional differences between males and females. For instance:

- Guys tend to give the emotional in order to receive the physical. They use romance to get sex. Girls typically give the physical in order to receive the emotional. They use sex to get romance.
- Emotionally, men move gradually and are either high or low (either happy or sad). Women can usually move between high and low much quicker.

- When it comes to affection, many men are like microwaves—ready for sex in seconds. Women, on the other hand, can take time to warm up; it's usually more of a process for them. Also, guys are often more visual, use their imagination, and are physically turned on. Women are often slower, more relational, and more emotionally turned on.

Some Helpful Questions to Answer

- "Are you who the person you are looking for is looking for?"[11] What are you doing to become this person?
- Where did your ideas of humanity, love, and sex come from? Are they from the right places and from people with wisdom and insight?
- How can you "make love" with someone you barely know?
- Why don't people ever talk about the fact that research shows that happily married couples have the most pleasurable sex lives together?
- Why doesn't our culture ever share the "end of the story" in TV shows or movies—the lives shipwrecked from pornography or sex outside of marriage?
- How far is too far? If you're hoping to get a checklist, you're going to be disappointed, but not totally. It's not like, *On date two, you can hold hands. Then on date five, you can make dinner together while giving each other a massage. Then on date eight, you can …* It doesn't work like that. The question should not be *how far is too far* but *how can you honor the person you are dating*? Asking "How far is too far?" is like asking "How far into the road can I stand before I get hit by the side-view mirror of a passing bus?"

Now for those of you who really need some ideas about how far is too far, one of my good friends, Mike, has three rules of thumb that might be helpful:

1. *If you can't talk about it, you can't do it.* Now that doesn't mean that if you *can* talk about it, you *can* do it. Good try.
2. *Lights on, clothes on, stay upright.* That's clear enough.
3. *Kissing, hugging, and holding hands, and that may be too far for some.* Now you might be mocking me for this, but it sure seems like problems begin when couples go beyond this.

THE UNSPOKEN EPIDEMIC

Pornography is a cancer. It's a silent killer. Access to porn is easier than ever, and more people view it than ever before. According to a recent study, more than 70 percent of men ages eighteen to thirty-four visit porn sites in a typical month. And it's not just guys watching sex online. It is estimated that one in three porn users today are women.[12]

Does all this really matter? Without a doubt. Psychology professor Dr. William Struthers says, "Viewing pornography is not an emotionally or physiologically neutral experience. It is fundamentally different from looking at black and white photos of the Lincoln Memorial or taking in a color map of the provinces of Canada. It is not a neutral stimulus. It draws us in. Porn is vicarious and voyeuristic at its core, but it is also something more. Porn is a whispered promise. It promises more sex, better sex, endless sex … experiences of transcendence demand."[13]

Does porn keep its promise? Not at all. In fact, pornography has been a silent assassin. It has ravaged and devastated people's love lives secretly for many years. Numerous studies have confirmed its effect on the human brain and on relationships. You need to stay away from porn. Not just so you can avoid roadblocks and pain, but so you can live with great joy. A porn-free life is about experiencing true freedom, security, and safety in relationships. It's not just about being *against* something; it's about being *for* something much better.

Effects of Porn

The negative effects of porn are many. Porn affects your brain, your dating life, your sex life, your marriage (present or future), your friendships, and your work. It creates a set of expectations about sex in marriage that are impossible to fulfill.

Here are what studies have found to be the effects: hostile sexism, more affairs, more divorce, lower sex quality, decreased sex drive, more difficulty with attention, and increased violence. Struthers says, "Men seem to be wired in such a way that pornography hijacks the proper functioning of their brains and has a long-lasting effect on their thoughts and lives."[14]

According to Dr. Syras Derksen, "There are many negative effects of pornography, but one of the most concerning aspects of pornography use is that users seem oblivious to how it is changing them."[15] And Ann Tolley adds, "Because this [pornography] is an addictive substance, it creates an appetite for itself. This appetite increases over time as you spend more and more time viewing pornography. The time spent viewing pornography can jeopardize work, relationships and interest in healthy pastimes. Over time the pornography we first started viewing becomes mundane. We feel an escalated desire to view things which we once would have considered as going too far or totally wrong."[16] With drug addiction, the body begins to "tolerate" the drug, so a bigger dosage is needed to get the same high. The same is true with porn. People become desensitized to what they're watching and need a bigger "dose" to become sexually aroused.

What to Do?

Struthers says, "Recovery is a neurological process, much as body building is a muscular process. Each time you view pornography, for example, you reinforce that neurological path. The intimacy developed in support and accountability groups can reinforce different, more virtuous, pathways in the brain. This can lead to intimacy not just along gender lines, but along generational lines as well."[17]

What can you do if you find yourself stuck in this pornography trap? How can you get out? Here are nine steps you can take to get out of the porn trap:

1. Tell at least two trusted friends of the same gender about your struggle and your desire to get free—maybe a pastor or mentor. Some of the power in porn is in its secrecy, guilt, and shame. You need to find someone to help you walk on this journey.

2. Learn about the pornography addiction. Be honest with yourself about how it's affecting you and your future. Begin with the future in mind. Actual meaningful relationships are better than porn. Decide to quit porn for life.

3. Get rid of all your porn. Throw away any movies or magazines and clear your computer. Unsubscribe from any porn websites.

4. Block all entry points. Get a software porn blocker such as Covenant Eyes or K-9 Web Protection. Android has a ton of options. iPhone can block all adult websites.

5. Identify and recognize your triggers and when you're more likely to use porn. Then find other (positive) ways to deal with these triggers. Rewrite your neuro-code. To break a habit, you must make a habit. Read *The Power of Habit* by Charles Duhigg for help.

6. Limit social media. Unfollow anyone who shares links, pics, or videos that are shady.

7. Identify alternative activities and hobbies that you can participate in.

8. Change your environment. Remove yourself from tempting locations.

9. Seek professional help (such as a therapist, counselor, pastor, addiction recovery program, or twelve-step support group) if you're not having the success you want in overcoming.

You can change your choices.
You can become the person you were meant to be.
You can make wise choices in this arena.
You can find fulfillment in agape relationships.

THE BIG 3

- Sex is designed to be enjoyed while married. If you wait for it, it will be worth it.

- Practice the Golden Rule of dating: Treat the person you're dating like you would want someone to treat your future spouse. Honor that person; he or she may become someone else's husband or wife.

- It's never too late to change your story.

PART 4

I WANT TO BE RICH

#C.R.E.A.M.
(CASH RULES EVERYTHING AROUND ME)

> *Work while they sleep.*
> *Learn while they party.*
> *Save while they spend.*
> *Then live like they dream.*
>
> —*Steve Canter, motivational coach, speaker, and blogger*

A whole $13,500. That was my (Pete's) starting salary my first year out of college. And I'm not that old. My paycheck after taxes were taken out was $888.13 monthly. That wasn't much money then, especially with my rent being $350. I'm not good with math (I was told there would be no math in this book), but I think that's $538.13 to live on for the *month*. And that doesn't count car insurance, utilities, and other bills.

It was rough. Grueling actually. And you know what? I wouldn't trade that time for the world. It taught me some great lessons. Hard lessons. But great ones. You can live on very little. You can live on peanuts. Literally peanuts. Not cashews or almonds (they're expensive) but actual in-shell Virginia peanuts. And grilled cheese. And Ramen. And PB&Js.

Then during my third year out of college, I hit the jackpot. My new salary was $21,000! Easy street. Poppin' bottles (of Cheerwine). Ballin'. Private jets. Right? Nope, it still made me eligible for subsidized housing. Those first three years showed me how blessed I actually was and how grateful I should be for even having a job. This was $8K more than I had made year one, so I thought I was living large. I told myself, *Well, I made it through last year making $8K less. I'm sure to make it this year.*

Not all my decisions were dripping with wisdom that year at age twenty-three, but I didn't blow the entire $8K. I saved a bunch more than the year before, and I started to develop habits that would build wealth over the long haul. It has paid off. Life is fun. You can treat other people, give away money that really makes a difference, and treat yourself from time to time.

WU-TANG CLAN WAS RIGHT

Cash rules everything around me (C.R.E.A.M). When the RZA, the JZA, Method Man, and ODB released this song in 1993 (my senior year of high school), they were prophetic. Cash was starting to rule everything. It still does. The desire for money and what money can provide drives our world. But what if we're looking at money the wrong way? What if the entire world is looking at money the wrong way?

Only two perspectives on money exist: abundance and scarcity. If you're reading this book, you're likely among the richest 2 percent in the world. If you drive your own car, you're definitely in the richest 1 percent. A couple of realities can help us gain perspective. Did you know that …

- Almost half of the world's population, more than 3 billion people, live on less than $2.50 a day ($75 a month).
- Almost one-quarter of all humans live without electricity. This is approximately 1.5 billion people.
- Eighty percent of the world's population lives on less than $10 a day.[1]

THE TWO PERSPECTIVES

1. **SCARCITY**: Total resource is limited; there's not enough for everyone; get yours while the gettin' is good; look out for yourself; make money any way you can; don't worry about integrity or right and wrong; stress, anxiety, worry; if someone else is making a lot, that means you must make a little.
2. **ABUNDANCE**: There is enough for everyone if you work for it; you reap what you sow; everyone can prosper; you can have peace

about money. Gratitude unlocks this attitude of abundance. How big is the pie for you? That is, the total amount of available resources. Some of this is determined by your background, your family, your experiences, etc. It is a mix of skill, circumstance, and effort.

We are rich. If you didn't worry about your next meal or water or shelter this past week, then you are rich. Why is it we worry and are so anxious about money? Let's change our mind-set. We have so much. We are so blessed. We should be so grateful. If you wake up and remind yourself of this each day, your outlook on money changes. Then you want to put your money to work. Doing good. In your life and in others' lives. Money can be a great joy in life or it can be an idol (something to worship). It can be a vice or it can be a catalyst for positive things. Your attitude toward money is a choice. Why not choose abundance?

HOW MUCH IS ENOUGH?

In his book *Enough: True Measures of Money, Business, and Life*, John C. Bogle says, "At a party given by a billionaire on Shelter Island, Kurt Vonnegut informs his pal, Joseph Heller, that their host, a hedge fund manager, had made more money in a single day than Heller had earned from his wildly popular novel *Catch-22* over its whole history. Heller responds, 'Yes, but I have something that he will never have … enough.'"[2] Enough. It's all you need.

How much money do you need to be happy? The latest studies put the tipping-point income at about $75,000 for a household. As income increased after that, happiness did not.[3] So what does this figure represent? Why $75,000?

I think this number is what most people need to not have to worry that when something breaks, they won't be able to fix it. More money doesn't equal more happiness. This is also demonstrated by how some of the wealthiest people in the world are also some of the most depressed. You might feel your economic situation is pressing down and suffocating you. Maybe the pressure feels unbearable. I've been there. But take courage. Billions of people have gone before you. And had worse stuff happen to them. And been in worse places financially. And had more student loans. And had more credit card debt. They've made it, and so can you. But not without some hard work. Are you up for it?

WILD TRUTH ALERT: YOU CAN BE A MILLIONAIRE!

You can be a millionaire. If you follow these simple steps. I guarantee it. That's the reality. I still work for that same nonprofit and make significantly less than most of my peers. But I'm on track to be a millionaire by age fifty-five. Maybe sooner. If you do these things and guard them ruthlessly, then it gets fun. Money can be a gift. Money can be fun. It just has to occupy the right place in your heart and life.

My average wage over the last twenty years of working has been $41,000. Average wage! This is very low for twenty years with the same company. And having a job every year. Many of you will have a starting salary right out of college that is more than this. Despite this low annual income, I have still been able to amass a significant net worth.

Net Worth = Assets - Liabilities

It's basically everything you own minus everything you owe. If someone who is making a relatively low wage and is as big a knucklehead as I am can do it, so can you! I promise. As C. S. Lewis said, "You can't go back and change the beginning, but you can start where you are and change the ending."

Everyone has a different starting point. You might have $100K or more in student loans. You might have no debt and a graduation gift of $10K to "start you out." You can't change your starting point right now, but you do have control over where you're going—the direction and the trajectory. That's the most important thing. How your family deals (or dealt) with money is a big factor in how you think about it.

Growing up, did you always feel like your family never had enough? Or on the flip side, did you never have to worry? Are you a spender or a saver? It's vital to know your tendencies so you can understand how to bring them in line with what you want to accomplish long term. I guarantee you that if you do these things, barring some weird catastrophic event or tragedy, you can become a millionaire before you retire.

Disclaimer: I am not a financial professional. I have never been to school for this. This is advice after much research and being with people in the corporate and nonprofit world for a while. So please take this all into consideration. This section is not meant to be a life guide on money. Don't be afraid to ask someone (or several people) you trust—a mentor, your parents, or a relative—about what they think. Maybe ask someone who seems to be successful at this, someone who is honest and has similar values to you. These are not hard and fast rules, they are meant to start you on your journey. But you will have to find your own way.

As theologian John Wesley said, "Earn all you can, save all you can and give all you can."[4]

The Secrets to Retiring as a Millionaire

1. Never go into debt. Ever. For any reason. (The only acceptable debt is a mortgage, and even that isn't great). If you already have some debt, treat it as a disease to be attacked ruthlessly and furiously. It's your financial enemy.
2. Automate your investing (we will talk more about this in another chapter). Set it and forget it. Look at it once or twice a year max.
3. Stop comparing. Social media image-crafting is crushing us. Does anyone ever post an ordinary or below-average day on Instagram, Facebook, etc.? This comparison game has no winners. In fact, every participant is a loser. Often after surfing around Instagram for a while, I feel like my life sucks. Don't compare.
4. Think about money the right way. It's not really yours. You're just a temporary steward of it. Do you hate money? Love it? Are you indifferent?
5. Have an attitude of abundance. Not scarcity. There is enough money for everyone to have a bunch.

6. Don't fear money. It's not evil. It can do a lot of good or a lot of bad depending on its caretaker. It can cause stress or it can relieve stress. It can discourage or encourage.

7. Get a plan and then work it! When you track your money, you begin to control the outcome. Organize your finances. Get it all down in the same place. Look at it from a fifty-thousand-feet view. Take inventory and get the big picture.

8. Spend less than you earn. The difference between the rich and poor is one cent. The rich make $1.00 and spend $0.99 and the poor make a $1.00 and spend $1.01.

9. Take the free money! Take advantage of any matches from your employers on any of your retirement accounts. Be sure to contribute at least the percent they match as your very first investment. No other investment doubles when you put money in.

10. Give generously and radically. This is almost impossible to do if you're in debt or just barely making ends meet. You reap what you sow. Sow generosity, then reap abundance.

11. Start as early as you can. Which is now. Seriously, today. Start saving today (see the next chapter for what to invest in). If you wait even a year, it can cost you tens of thousands of dollars on the back end.

12. Have a long-term view. Make good decisions and let time help you. Don't let long-term plans based on short-term events or news rattle you or cause you to make impulsive decisions. Slow and steady wins the race.

13. Take financial advisor Bryan Rex's advice: "When you are flying from Boston to Los Angeles, does the pilot hop on the speaker telling you of the storm happening in Kansas? Nope. Or of the snowstorm in Chicago? Do you get upset because you did not pack a coat? Nope, because you are not going to Chicago, that news is not relevant to *your* long-term plan. Today's 24-hour news cycle and main-lined social media intake is like inviting every passenger into the cockpit on a plane. You will likely hear a

lot of alarming news that is not really that alarming but sure feels like it when processed through the perspective of those who are not professional pilots."[5]

14. Look for ways to increase your income. Diversification is not just for your investments. Look for ways to earn extra money—freelance, work on weekends, use the skills you have, sell stuff around your house, etc. Or just grind it out and do some hard things early when you're young and you have the time, energy, and stamina. While I was in college, I gave piano lessons to Norm and Andrew, a father/son duo. It was fun and gave me some needed extra income.

15. Treat every paycheck the same. The formula for success is located in the next chapter.

One word on failure: Bounce back quickly from it. Failure is okay. Even business magnate Warren Buffett makes a mistake now and then. You can rally back. Except if you invest all your money in some weird new technology. Or a "startup fund." Or your friend's "exclusive market-changing product." Don't do that.

Now here's some bonus advice to make things fun: Celebrate along the way. When you reach milestones and bigger accomplishments, please stop and celebrate. Make saving fun.

WORK ALL THE ANGLES

If you're just starting out, maybe you're reading this in your senior year of high school or in college. Great! Did you know that fewer than two out of five millennials negotiate their first salary? That means that they start on their employer's terms. Most companies don't want to overpay or overspend for young, fresh-out-of-college employees. Most companies will offer a salary on the lower side.

Now some salaries are not negotiable but most are. You must negotiate this incredibly important starting point. According to *Time* magazine, "80% of those who ask for a bump actually get some—if not all—of the money they request. Plus, 76% of hiring managers say candidates who negotiate appear more confident for doing so."[6]

So this money thing is like the *Who Wants to Be a Millionaire?* game show. If you follow the rules, make wise decisions, ask advice from the right people, and are willing to work hard at it, you can do it. In the next chapter, we'll take you through practical steps and exactly what to do with your money.

THE BIG 3

♦ Thou shalt spend less than you earn. Maybe way less. (Debt is the enemy.)

♦ Thou shalt start now. Like today. Seriously, put it on your to-do list today. Or yesterday.

♦ Thou shalt give generously. You reap what you sow. Sow some good seeds.

9

#BUDGETINGBASICS

It's not your salary that makes you rich,
it's your spending habits.
—*Charles A. Jaffe, finance author*

Y ou want to be rich? You don't have to make a lot of money (and you probably won't in your first job). You do have to be wise with what you have. And how do you do that? A budget. I know, I know. A budget is that annoying thing your parents had that kept you from buying stuff or going on a vacation. Anytime you wanted anything, you were met with the line, "That's not in the budget." *Ahhh! Stupid budget,* you thought. *When I get my own money, I'll do anything I want with it.*

So here you are. An adult. A real person with a real job making real money. How rich do you feel? Or do you look at your bank account and wonder where it all went? Do you know how much you spent on food last month? Or did that movie ticket make you overdraft your bank account?

Read up. What you are about to learn will save you a lifetime of frustration. If you can learn to budget well when you're young, you will never be poor. John C. Maxwell says, "A budget is telling your money where to go instead of wondering where it went."[1]

So where do you even start? Glad you asked. The first thing you need to do is figure out how much money you get in your paycheck (after taxes). You want to be sure that you never owe money on April 15 (tax day). But you also don't want a huge refund. You want to never have a surprise on this day. The way you avoid surprises is by properly filling out your deductions on your W-9 form (the document that tells your employer how much money to take out of your paycheck) and using a good accountant (or computer software).

Here's what to do:

1. Figure out how much money you make.
2. Give 10 percent. This can go to a church, charity, or any organization that supports others in need. If you can learn generosity while you make a little, then you won't have a hard time being generous when you make a lot.
3. Pay yourself. Immediately shave off 15 percent of your income and place it into a savings account. This is money you can't touch. You want to build these habits young. You will learn in the next chapter how investing a little early will make you a lot of money later (and where to invest this money).
4. At this point you should have 75 percent of what you originally made. Now how much do you *need*? Not need like a new outfit need, but absolute essentials. Use 10 percent to pay down debt and the other 65 percent is what you use to budget. This includes housing, food, car, phone, utilities. Pull out all your bills and figure out what you need for survival. Anything else is a luxury.
5. Get out a piece of paper, open an Excel spreadsheet, or use anything else that will help you create a budget. Running through the numbers in your head does you no good at all. You need to see them on paper.
6. Write out your categories. For most people, this will be similar but have small variances.
7. Write down what you make. Now write down where you want to spend.
8. Ensure that you give, pay yourself first, and take care of the essentials. The rest is yours. Go crazy. Why not? You have done the most critical part. If you're giving and saving, then you're free to spend everything else. There's freedom within boundaries. Warren Buffet says, "Do not save what is left after spending, but spend what is left after saving."[2]

A SAMPLE BUDGET

Below is a sample budget that I (Josh) use with young people all the time. (Note that these numbers change dramatically depending on where you live. The example below is just that, an example.)

	MONTHLY BUDGET	JANUARY	FEBRUARY
Income	2,500		
Give	250		
Save	375		
Expenses			
Insurance	100		
Rent	500		
Auto			
Insurance	80		
Gas	100		
Service & Parts	50		
Cell Phone	50		
Electric Bill	100		
Internet / Cable	50		
Entertainment	100		
Groceries	150		
Restaurants	75		
Gifts	50		
Health	50		
Clothes	50		
Miscellaneous	50		
TOTAL EXPENSES	1,555		
Margin (Income-Giving-Saving-Expenses)	320		

This is not supposed to be tricky or difficult. Being rich is simply spending less than you earn. Being poor is spending more than you earn. This is true regardless of what you earn.

There is a young woman who has been working at my restaurant for a little while now, and she earns $11 an hour. She isn't making some crazy six-figure income, but she just finished paying off her car. Not a cheap $500 car, but a nice $15,000 vehicle that she went out and earned all on her own. She knew how much she made, was wise in her spending, and paid off her car several years early because she budgeted well.

Contrast this with another one of my young employees. This individual asked me to sit down with him and assess if he had enough money to move out on his own. We sat down and talked through his income, current life expenses, cost of school, and everything else. At the end of the conversation, I looked him in the eye and said, "The numbers don't lie. What you're trying to do doesn't work right now. Perhaps once you're out of school and can work more hours. Or if you had fewer other expenses in your life. But moving out on your own will only cause frustration because the numbers don't work."

Fast forward three months and this young man moved out anyway. I guess he expected more money to just appear or thought he could change his poor spending habits. Neither happened. He was miserable because he didn't budget correctly and spent more than he made.

Follow the Plan

We have talked about building a budget, but that doesn't do you any good unless you follow it. Anyone can make a pretty spreadsheet that tells them what to do. But only if you actually follow this will it happen. So how do you follow your exciting new budget?

- Use a system to track purchases. Place the cash amount in envelopes and when you run out of money, you're done. Or use an online system that connects to your debit card such as Mint.com or YNAB (You Need a Budget). These help you categorize your money so you can see where it's going.

- Review your budget frequently. Organize your expenses daily and know how much money you have remaining in each account. If you don't track, you will never know.
- Ask other people to help you. In our society, money is taboo to talk about. But why on earth should you not discuss money? If you want to be held to a budget, share that budget with other people who can help you. There is nothing better than having someone hold you accountable.

As former vice president Joe Biden said, "Don't tell me what you value. Show me your budget, and I'll tell you what you value."[3] Money management doesn't have to be hard. This is something you can control. It doesn't need to control you.

THE BIG 3

- Spend less than you make.
- Create a budget.
- Follow the budget.

#LITTLEHINGES

Would you rather have a penny that doubles in value every day for thirty days or $10,000 every day for thirty days?

Many of you know the answer to this classic riddle, but the answer is shown on the following page.

After ten days, if you took the side of the penny, you're looking pretty ridiculous. It's only worth $5 compared to $100,000. It's not even close. But by day twenty-six, you have already surpassed the person who thought $10,000 a day was better. By the end of the thirty days, one person is a multi-millionaire and the other has $300,000. This illustration is intended to show you the power of investing and the principal of compounding interest. It doesn't matter how much you earn. What matters is how early you invest.

Before we dive any deeper into investing, it's critical to understand a few of the terms that we will be using. If you don't know what an asset or liability is, then this chapter will be worthless. Let's begin our financial journey by clearly outlining the language we'll use (how to use each these items will be discussed throughout the chapter). This chapter exists to begin walking you through the beginning steps of understanding and maximizing your finances.

- *Checking Account*: An account with a bank or financial institution that holds the money you use for expenses.
- *Savings Account*: An account held with a bank or financial institution that holds the money that you save for emergencies or the future.

PENNY VS. $10,000

DAY	$0.01	$10,000.00
1	$0.01	$10,000.00
2	$0.02	$20,000.00
3	$0.04	$30,000.00
4	$0.08	$40,000.00
5	$0.16	$50,000.00
6	$0.32	$60,000.00
7	$0.64	$70,000.00
8	$1.28	$80,000.00
9	$2.56	$90,000.00
10	$5.12	$100,000.00
11	$10.24	$110,000.00
12	$20.48	$120,000.00
13	$40.96	$130,000.00
14	$81.92	$140,000.00
15	$163.84	$150,000.00
16	$327.68	$160,000.00
17	$655.36	$170,000.00
18	$1310.72	$180,000.00
19	$2621.44	$190,000.00
20	$5242.88	$200,000.00
21	$10,485.76	$210,000.00
22	$20,971.52	$220,000.00
23	$41,943.04	$230,000.00
24	$83,886.08	$240,000.00
25	$167,772.16	$250,000.00
26	$335,544.32	$260,000.00
27	$671,088.64	$270,000.00
28	$1,342,177.28	$280,000.00
29	$2,684,354.56	$290,000.00
30	$5,368,709.12	$300,000.00

- *Assets*: Anything that you own that has value. Examples include a car, a home, stocks, etc.
- *Liability*: Anything that you owe. Debt is a liability because you owe something to someone else. Examples include a car loan, mortgage, credit card debt, etc.
- *Stocks*: A piece of a company that you can own. Did you know that you can buy a piece of Disney or Coca-Cola?
- *Mutual Funds*: A collection of stocks that you can buy into. This method gives you diversification. Diversification allows you to spread your money throughout several different companies so you can minimize your risk.
- *Principal*: The amount of money that interest is based on. If you have a mortgage on a home for $100,000, the $100,000 is the principal amount, and the interest due each month is based on how much of that original $100,000 is still owed. This will be shown in greater detail in the chapter about buying a house.
- *Interest*: The amount you pay someone else for borrowing money. You pay interest whenever you buy a house. You borrow money from a bank, and the bank "charges" you each month based on how much money you borrowed.
- *401(k)*: A defined contribution plan where employees make contributions from their paycheck that go into a retirement account. The employee can often choose the investments within the company's 401(k) plan offering. The crazy name is based on a line of tax code from the 1980s that governs how this retirement plan is managed.

This chapter will give you the *why* behind investing, and the upcoming chapters will talk more about how to invest. Before you can do any kind of investing, you need to have your money accessible in a financial institution. You need a checking *and* a savings account. Just about every bank out there offers some type of free checking account. This is what you want. Never pay a bank to hold your money. They need you more than you need them. Don't forget that.

Go to your local bank and open a checking account and a savings account now if you don't have them already. Literally, put down this book and go do it. Don't worry about high-yield savings accounts or anything else. But beware, banks are for-profit institutions. They will try to sell you all kinds of stuff, like credit cards, "better" accounts, lines of credit, etc. Refuse it all except for a free checking account and savings account.

So what do you do with each account? Are they different?

The first and most frequently used is the checking account. This account is what you should use (not a credit card) for your day-to-day expenses. Do you need gas for your car? Use your bank debit card. Do you need groceries? Use your bank debit card. Do you want to go to the movies? Use your bank debit card. Never use a credit card until you have a strong understanding of only spending after giving and saving. We will talk more about this later on.

By using a bank debit card, you will only spend money that you already have. By using a credit card, it is much easier to fall into the trap of "I can just pay it back later." This is a lie. Ask anyone in their thirties or forties who has credit card debt if it was worth it. I bet they will all say no.

Now that you'll be using a bank debit card and have your money securely in a bank, we can move forward with investing.

BIG DOORS SWING ON LITTLE HINGES

There's a "little hinge" in the finance world that has unbelievable impact. It's the "ninja of finance." It's something that's moving around silently, behind the scenes and almost undetected, but changing outcomes in a huge way. It is a juggernaut, an unstoppable force, and has nuclear-type energy. We call it compound interest.

Investopedia defines compound interest as "interest calculated on the initial principal and also on the accumulated interest of previous periods of a deposit or loan."[1] In other words, it is interest on interest. The interest you earn in one period is then added to the original amount invested (principal), and then you earn interest in the next period on both principal (original investment) *and* the most recent interest. That's a lot of words. Let me show you what I mean.

The Power of Compound Interest

Example: You start investing $200/month at age twenty-five. This is $2,400 per year, which is 10 percent of a yearly salary of $24,000. (Most of you will make much more than this. If you're not, please reevaluate your job or ask for a raise.) You invest this amount every month until age sixty-five.

Investing $200/month until age sixty-five ($2,400 per year), and assuming an 8 percent return, at age sixty-five, you'll have an account in which you have put a total of $98,400 of your own money. But the actual total in the account is ... wait for it ... $673,874! How did I come up with this number? Look at the table on the following page.

Where did that 8 percent number come from? How is my money growing? Does it happen automatically? 8 percent is the common number used to project growth over a long period. The lowest return in the history of the stock market for a 20-year period is over 6 percent. Even if you include the years of the Great Depression. The average rate used by many financial advisors for projecting market growth is 8 percent.

Most of you reading this will be on the younger side. Probably in your twenties. Compound interest will be your best friend. You have an incredible opportunity in front of you. You have the opportunity to let time be your friend. Your ally. Your confidant. You may be just starting in your job and thinking you want to settle in and wait to see what happens with your money situation. Maybe you want to wait a year to get your feet under you, get your head on straight, or get a handle on your finances. This would be a grave mistake. Let me show you how much waiting even five years could cost you.

Now let's say you wait five years to start investing. What if you wait till age thirty to start instead of twenty-five? The account value at age sixty-five will be $449,045—a difference of $224,829. For just waiting five years! Almost a quarter of a million dollars. For just waiting five years and not putting in that measly $10,000 over those years. Crazy, right?

AGE	INVESTED YEARLY	FINAL TOTAL
25	$2,400	$2,400
26	2,400	4,992
27	2,400	7,791
28	2,400	10,815
29	2,400	14,080
30	2,400	17,606
31	2,400	21,415
32	2,400	25,528
33	2,400	29,970
34	2,400	34,768
35	2,400	39,949
36	2,400	45,545
37	2,400	51,589
38	2,400	58,116
39	2,400	65,165
40	2,400	72,778
41	2,400	81,001
42	2,400	89,881
43	2,400	99,471
44	2,400	109,829
45	2,400	121,015
46	2,400	133,096
47	2,400	146,144
48	2,400	160,235
49	2,400	175,454
50	2,400	191,891
51	2,400	209,642
52	2,400	228,813
53	2,400	249,518
54	2,400	271,880
55	2,400	296,030
56	2,400	322,112
57	2,400	350,281
58	2,400	380,704
59	2,400	413,560
60	2,400	449,045
61	2,400	487,369
62	2,400	528,758
63	2,400	573,459
64	2,400	621,736
65	2,400	673,874
Total	**$98,400**	**$673,874**

WHAT ARE YOU WAITING FOR?

This should compel you to start saving now! According to *Forbes*, 63 percent of Americans fail to save any money after paying their bills.[2] And many are going further and further in debt every month. Start investing now. Even if it's $25 per month. Set up automatic deductions.

Your employer can help you with this. If you are getting direct deposit from work into your bank account, you can split that money. Instead of 100 percent of your paycheck going into checking, you can have them automatically send a portion of it to your savings account. You can't spend what you don't have in your checking account, so put your money where you want it to go and you'll be shocked at your resourcefulness to make what you have leftover work.

I've told you that in my first year out of college I (Pete) made $13,500. I visited a recommended financial planner, and the amount I wanted to invest per month was so low his computer software wasn't even able to calculate it. The minimum it was set up to start with was more than I was going to invest per month, and he had to do my projections by hand. But I started. I got in the game. You should too.

Okay, so you're convinced that compound interest is more powerful than if Arnold Schwarzenegger and Chuck Norris had a child. Now what? You can't invest if you don't have anything. Let's look at some tips and tricks to save some money. Then in the next chapter we'll look at how to invest the money that you're saving.

TOP 10 WAYS TO ACTUALLY SAVE MONEY NOW

1. Warning. Repetition for emphasis coming: *Spend less than you make.* Live within your means.
2. Warning. Repetition for emphasis coming: *Avoid debt at all cost.* If you already have some, the next chapter gives a systematic way to get out of debt.
3. Write down your financial goals. Where do you want to be in one year, five years, ten years, and at the end of your life? What do

you want to have accomplished? There is power in writing things down and seeing them. Review them regularly.

4. Don't go "shopping." Think of yourself as a member of the SWAT team retail division. You go in, take care of business, and get out. These are tactical strikes and not for fun. Don't look through catalogs that you don't need products from. Don't browse in stores where you don't need anything.

5. Use things until they fall apart. Make it a contest to see how long you can use something (not when it's a matter of safety—come on, we're not savages).

6. Spend more time shopping for a bigger purchase. If you save $20 and it took you 20 minutes, you just paid yourself $60/hour, but if you saved $20 and it took you 4 hours, you just paid yourself $5/hour.

7. Shop for Christmas and birthday presents year-round. If you find something that's an incredible deal, buy it and keep it in a box. Anticipate and stay organized.

8. Don't start a tab. When you're out for drinks, pay for all the drinks when you order them unless you want to spend much more than you expect. Also know that eating out is expensive. Often with the tip and tax, it can be 30 percent more than the price on the menu. Doesn't it happen all the time that you get the bill at a restaurant and think, *Wow, that's way more than I thought!*

9. Have an email account for all those discount restaurant clubs and frequent visitor points. Search it for coupons when you are at that merchant.

10. Ironic, counterintuitive twist: Give away some money. Be generous. Tip extravagantly. You reap what you sow.

SOME TIPS AND TRICKS

At the Grocery Store

- Price per unit is the most important thing at the grocery store.

- Philosophy of coupons: Don't spend a lot of time with them. Have a cheesy email address that you sign up for all the clubs and discounts with (see #9 above). Then search it if you're going somewhere with one of those "very important customer" clubs. Make sure if you spend time "clipping," that it's worth it. What hourly rate are you paying yourself?
- Make an electronic grocery list on your phone. Add to it the things you need, and don't buy other things.
- Never grocery shop when you're hungry.
- Don't be afraid to try non-name brand varieties. Some taste just as good. And they are usually signficantly cheaper.
- Check your top four or five favorite foods or products every time you go. If they're on sale, stock up.
- Make a big meal for the whole week. A little in the fridge, a little in the freezer.
- How you eat will be determined at the grocery store. Do you want to eat healthy? Also, if you don't have anything to eat at home, the quickest remedy is usually the least healthy (and often more expensive).
- Use a pickup system if your grocery store offers this feature. Shop online and pick up at the store. This saves time and money. Even if there's a cost for this service, it will help prevent you from buying unnecessary items.
    + Other tips from my dear friend Aimee:
    + Plan your meals around what's on sale and in season. Use the weekly store ad to help you find what's on sale. Usually these are online.
- Try out lower-cost chains like Aldi and Marc's. Often they have even better deals per unit cost than wholesale clubs like Costco.

At Clothing Stores

I used to dress sloppily. In high school and college, my style was big, baggy, and oversized. When I entered the real world, I worked with someone named Christin. One day she boldly asked me why I didn't wear clothes that fit. I replied that I got most of my stuff from clearance racks at Marshalls and TJ Maxx (both great stores). She explained to me the "baller outfit" principle—and I am eternally grateful.

Christin made me go shopping with her at Banana Republic at the mall. I had never been in that store and never gotten any clothes at the mall. Ever. When I saw a shirt for $55, I laughed heartily. She explained that it's better to have a couple "baller outfits" that fit well and you can't wait to wear than to have ten pieces of clothing that don't fit right but you got much cheaper. So I discovered the Banana Republic Outlet clearance section. This means you can get great-looking clothes that fit for a reasonable price. But get a couple of baller outfits—especially a nice suit or a couple of nice dresses that you can wear time and time again.

DON'T LET MONEY MAKE YOU EMOTIONAL

Be careful of the emotional side of money. Spending, budgeting, and saving are emotional. We must disassociate ourselves from it. Some of these things seem to be small and insignificant. Let me give you an example.

Let's say you get a grande soy two-pump no whip caramel macchiato on the way to work three times per week. And maybe one on the weekend. So that's four times per week, $5 per drink = $20 per week x 52 = $1,040 per year. If you just took half of that, which is $520, and invested it in an account that averaged 8 percent for thirty years, you would end up with $62,568. Now I'm not saying you shouldn't have some fancy coffees from time to time, but just know that it's a significant cost over the long haul. And time is on your side. Something small done repeatedly over a long period of time ends up being big.

Okay, so you've gotten some good habits to save some money. What do you do with it?

THE BIG 3

- Compounding interest is your friend.
- Spend less than you earn and avoid debt at all costs.
- Start saving and investing now. Right this minute.

#STILLEATINGRAMENAT70

Have you ever seen a hearse pulling a U-Haul? I (Pete) mentioned this in chapter 1. It bears repeating. Naked you come, naked you go. You can't take your money with you. It all goes to someone else when you die. And you will die. The death rate is holding steady at one per person. So the sooner you can figure out that you're a temporary steward, the more freedom you'll experience. We're all temporary managers of our money and resources. So let's try to do the most good for the most people. And have some fun along the way.

In the *30 for 30* episode "Broke," ESPN chronicles professional athletes who make staggering amounts of money and after a few years out of sports declare bankruptcy. According to a 2009 *Sports Illustrated* article, 60 percent of NBA players are broke within five years of retiring from basketball. By the time they've been retired for two years, 78 percent of former NFL players have gone bankrupt or are under financial stress.[1] These people are in the upper 1 percent of earners in the country. It's not just a matter of how much money you make but what you do with it.

In your parents' and grandparents' days, the traditional pension plan bore the lion's share of saving. A pension is an investment account that your employer puts money in for your retirement, in addition to your salary. Most people depended on it. That has gone the way of MySpace. Pensions have mostly disappeared. Social Security is on life support, and with so much uncertainty around it, it cannot be depended on for your retirement livelihood. So guess who is on the hook for preparing for and investing for their own retirement? You got it. You!

But this also has its advantages. If you start early (which you can) and set some things up automatically, you can leverage time to be your biggest ally. Your plan is also completely customizable. You can invest in anything you want.

As the old song (and movie) goes, money can't buy you love. Or happiness. But learning to manage it wisely will save you a whole lot of trouble. In college, the concept of being smart with money translated to calculating how much Chipotle I could consume while still using every meal/punch on the meal plan. "Guac or no guac? It's extra? I know. Give me as much as you're allowed to." Looking at my college bills was about the same as playing a game of Monopoly or Life. Money had very little meaning or value. It was a game of survival and immediate gratification. If I wanted something, I directed all my resources to getting it. ASAP. But now … it's real life.

We've talked about the philosophy around money. We've talked about principles for becoming a millionaire. And we've talked about how to save money. But what do you actually *do* with your money?

Reminder: I am not a financial professional. I have spoken with many and asked what their advice would be and this is a compilation, but please make your own decisions.

RECOMMENDED INVESTMENT ORDER

1. Set up a matching 401(k) (or any matching money from your employer). Put in the maximum that your employer matches. It's free money. There are no other investments that double upon putting your money in the investment vehicle. Example: If your employer will match up to 4 percent of your salary that you contribute to your 401(k) (or any savings plan), put at least that amount in. It's like an automatic raise.

2. Save $1,000 as quickly as possible in something liquid (easily accessible), like a checking account. Make this a different account than your everyday checking account. You don't want to be tempted that the new iPad is on sale and that's an "emergency."

3. Now you have some options depending on your situation. If you have no debt except for a mortgage, proceed to step five. If you have some debt, then proceed with step 4.

4. Get out of debt. Attack it ruthlessly. Go after it. Most likely your first enemy target is credit card debt. Then your next one is probably a car payment. Maybe think about selling your car, paying the whole thing off, and buying a less expensive car with cash. Make sure to check whether there are early repayment penalties. Then possibly student loans are your next target. (We'll look at more information on paying off debt later in this chapter.)

5. Roth IRA. IRA = Individual Retirement Account. This is "after-tax" money—that is, income that you've already paid taxes on. But the benefit is that it grows tax free. The maximum contribution amount has changed over time. As of 2017, it was $5,500 per person. The easiest way to find the current maximum contribution is to Google it. Fight to put the maximum in. If you can't, put in as much as you can. For the long term, tax-free growth will be an incredible benefit.

6. Build that $1,000 fund from step two into an "emergency fund" of about three to six months' worth of expenses. Not expenses including Netflix and lattes. Just the essentials of what you need to survive, including housing costs, car payment, utilities, gas, insurance, and food. Don't touch this except in true emergencies.

7. Start your car fund. Even with a small amount. I put this transfer into a money market fund. A money market is almost like a checking account. Because I'm thinking that the car fund will be a shorter-term investment (five to ten years), it earns a much lower interest rate (usually like 0 percent) than most stocks, but it is much safer. If you have an accident, you might be emptying the account, and you don't want to be forced to cash out on a market downturn.

8. Once you have steps one to six mastered, as you have more money available, then you can invest more. Our recommenda-

tion is to put equal parts into the three funds mentioned later in this chapter.

So when you invest all this money for different purposes, what fund should you choose? The longer term the investment, the more aggressive the mutual fund you should choose. Remember, a mutual fund is a collection of stocks and bonds. You use a mutual fund to diversify your investments and reduce risk. Many people use index funds as a core and then build around them.

An index fund is created to match the overall performance of an index. It provides large-market exposure with minimal costs. An index is a measure for groups of stocks. One of the most common is the Dow Jones Industrial Average, which is made up of thirty of the largest and most influential companies in America. There are also the Nasdaq, NYSE, Russell 2000, and many more. Each index monitors different segments of the overall stock market.

Each person needs to diagnose their own risk tolerance. There are ways to do this online or by speaking with a financial professional whom you trust. If you are young and healthy, go as aggressive as you can stand. These are not accounts you should be checking every week. I check my investments about every six months and reallocate if I need to. Plan for this money to be in there for a long time.

Find someone you trust to discuss these decisions. This could be your parents (if they have been successful investors and are knowledgeable) or maybe a friend of the family.

DEBT CORNER: HOW TO PAY OFF DEBT

A couple of weeks ago, I was with several of my old students. They were talking about new jobs and money and finances. One young woman shared that she had paid for her entire undergrad degree with student loans (around $130,000). Her payment is around $1,300 per month, which is almost double the mortgage payment on my first house.

So what does she do? Is she beyond the point of no return? No. She's not on easy street, but she is really sharp and is going to go after it with everything she has.

Two Debt Repayment Methods: Snowball and Ladder

Snowball and ladder: each has its advantages. Snowball is more psychological, and the ladder is for math nerds. (I majored in math for my freshman year in college, so I'm allowed to call you a math nerd. I'm one too. So relax. Go do a differential equation.) Most people should utilize the snowball method, which we'll explain first.

First thing to do is get a handle on what you owe. Get everything in one place. Make a list of each debt, including the balance owed, interest rate, and monthly minimum payment. There are a bunch of worksheets available online to help. You can find them by googling "debt repayment plan worksheet." There should be several free ones as the first ones listed.

Next find out how much you have each month to pay off debt. Suspend all credit card use to avoid "new" interest and keep track of everything you spend for two weeks. Every transaction! Now estimate your expenses for the month and add the minimum payment on every balance. Now add 25 percent to that number and figure out a way to come up with it. Focus all your energy (and money) on one debt—either the one with the highest interest rate (ladder method) or the one with the smallest balance (snowball method).

For the ladder method, start with the debt with the highest interest rate and pay it off. Then go to the balance with the next highest interest rate and so on. For the snowball method, start with the debt of the smallest balance and pay it off. Then go to the next smallest balance and so on.

Tips for Paying Off Debt

1. Pay off your credit cards first.
2. Don't incur any new credit card debt. Be ruthless. Don't charge anything new. In fact, you might need to cut up your credit cards.
3. Don't pay the "minimum." This is terrible. Pay the maximum you can afford.

4. Car loans are usually not good. Think about selling your car, paying off that loan, and buying a cheaper car using cash.
5. Student loans and mortgages are the only debt you should even entertain, but don't. Pay them off as well.
6. Look at increasing your income or, if you are a two-income household, try living on one and paying debt off with the other.
7. Celebrate along the way. When you finish a debt, treat yourself and a friend to a nice dinner. But pay cash. Don't charge it.

Dave Ramsey has great wisdom on paying off debt. His book *Total Money Makeover* has helped many people. Or, if you want to dive a little deeper, look into Financial Peace University (available on DVD and through some churches and other organizations). Definitely consider these if you're not going to do any of the stuff we just recommended.

Super Simplified Strategy

- Pay off debt first.
- Create an emergency fund.
- Take 15 percent of your salary (as mentioned in budgeting chapter to put towards savings). Put it in a 401(k) plan, an IRA, or a taxable account. Invest equal amounts of your 15 percent (5 percent each) into three different mutual funds:
  - S&P 500 index tracking fund (for example, Vanguard's S&P 500 fund ticker symbol SPY)
  - A U.S. total stock market index fund (for example, Dow Jones)
  - An international total stock market index fund
- Readjust each year to have equal amounts in all three as they will grow at different rates. You readjust in one of two ways: either by speaking with the person managing your money or manually online. And increase the percentage that you are saving by at least the inflation rate (approximately 3.25 percent each year).

- Take 10 percent and pay down debt.
- Give 10 percent away.
- Live on the other 65 percent.

ONE LAST WORD

Think long term. Set it and basically forget about it. Once you are established, give yourself (and your spouse and kids) grace. Splurge here and there. Don't wait to spend all your saved money till you're too old to enjoy it. Celebrate along the way and do things that you want to because you've been wise. Be generous. Diversify (don't put all your eggs in one basket). Do the most good for the most people. Set up your investments as automatic deductions. Then live on what's left. You can do it!

THE BIG 3

- Take massive action to get out of debt.
- Always take free money.
- When in doubt, use an S&P 500 index fund (SPY), a U.S. total stock market index fund, and an international total stock market index fund for diversification in investing.

PART 5

HOW TO NOT LOSE AT THE GAME OF MONEY

#NEVERPAYTHESTICKER

David really loved nice cars. Not nice like newish Toyota Camry nice. Nice, like BMW nice. He was one of those kids who was too cool for school, walked with some swagger, and rocked one of those fauxhawk haircuts (and occasionally a man bun). He had just graduated from high school and was figuring out what was next in life when he came to work at my restaurant.

I (Josh) got to know David and really began to understand his passion about new cars. For him, it was a sign of success and proof that he really mattered as a person. As a high school senior, he was already driving a BMW. When I was a senior in high school, I drove a 1995 Ford Windstar minivan. I think my parents were playing some kind of cruel joke on me, but I can't know for sure. Maybe they just wanted to ensure that I couldn't get a date.

One day, David came in and informed me of the brand-new Chevy Camaro he wanted to buy. It was going to set him back about $40,000.

Now it goes without saying that most eighteen-year-olds probably don't bring in enough money to pay for this kind of status symbol. And before any of my student-aged team members purchase a vehicle, I try to sit down with them and talk through it with them. I want to make sure they're not making a rash decision because their friend just got a new car. I've seen that all too often—a person going out and ignorantly spending way too much money on a new ride. They then take it down to the rim shop and lease (yes, you read that right) a new set of rims.

You can probably guess what happens now. Without properly thinking about their actual income and the added expenses of a new car, they quickly have the car repossessed. Not a big deal until you realize the long-term effects that it has on your credit.

PLAN AND PREPARE

There are many factors that go into the decision-making process when buying a car. Don't be like the person who immediately had the car repossessed because they didn't plan well. Yes, the sticker price is important, but it's just one of the components to consider. Before making any kind of large purchase, always consult with someone you trust who is financially responsible and has made a similar purchase. Here are the major drivers of cost *after* the purchase price:

- Insurance
- Taxes
- Maintenance
- Gas

DUPED BY A "DEAL"

The car-buying experience can be extremely overwhelming—and deceiving—unless you're prepared. For example, one evening, my wife and I decided to go check out some cars. We were newly married, had no money to our names, and just wanted to go browse. We weren't looking to buy a vehicle. We wound up at a Ford dealership near our home on a gorgeous fall night, walking around looking at all the beautiful new vehicles that we couldn't afford. Both of our cars had over 150,000 miles on them, but we weren't nearly prepared to purchase a different vehicle. (I have learned that the cheapest car you will ever own is the one you've already paid off).

We were minding our own business when a salesperson approached. We didn't really want any help (we weren't going to buy anything), but the salesman kept talking to us. He told us that since it was getting close to the end of the year, all the existing year's vehicles were on sale. We could get a "killer deal" if we wanted to purchase one now. We said, "We're not interested," but he was persistent.

Fast forward an hour, and my wife and I were driving off the lot in a gorgeous, fully loaded, brand new $45,000 F-150 King Ranch truck. This was the truck that dreams are made of. I couldn't believe it. The salesman had convinced us to take it home for the weekend for a "test drive." We hadn't purchased it yet, but he knew that we wouldn't want to give it up.

I drove away and felt like I was on top of the world. *Will every day feel like this moment?* I thought. It had that new car smell and was jacked up so that I was higher than everyone else on the road. This was a far cry from my first mid-'90s minivan and my current decade-old sedan. I suddenly had to have this truck.

The next morning, we did some math and realized that we would be broke for the next six years if I bought this truck. Here I was, a new business owner, and I was duped by the oldest car-buying tricks in the book. Let me tell you a secret: Dealers are always having sales. Just turn on your TV during any sporting event. I was nearly suckered into a debt that I would have been miserable with for years. I sadly returned the truck the next morning, jumped back in my twelve-year-old car, and drove away.

How did it get to this point? I didn't even want to buy a vehicle twenty-four hours before. I was just looking, and I almost got into six years of debt for a car I never wanted. Now my old sedan would never be enough.

Sadly, this is far too often the way a car-buying experience feels. You go in with certain expectations and hopes but walk away feeling defeated, overwhelmed, and confused.

KNOW BEFORE YOU GO

So what can you do? How do you defend against this? The first question to ask yourself is, *Do I even* need *a new vehicle and, if so, can I afford it?* We always want a newer vehicle, but is it necessary? If the answer is yes, then the biggest factor is simply understanding the way the numbers work and how you can negotiate the best deal.

First, let's dissect the costs associated with a purchase of an automobile. You have the sticker price, the taxes paid to the government that aren't reflected on that sticker, and the cost of the tags so you can drive the vehicle. You can't get the tags without proof of insurance. If you're financing a car, you must have full insurance coverage, not just liability (we'll talk more about that later). And if it's a specialty vehicle or something with expensive parts, you need to add that to the overall cost of purchasing and maintaining a vehicle.

The average annual cost to own a sedan is nearly $8,500. Included in this is depreciation, maintenance, repair, and fuel costs.[1] This doesn't even include insurance or taxes. The insurance amount is much higher for a student (but ask your insurance agent for a student discount or safe driver discount). It's easy to see just the sticker price and assume that you can afford a vehicle. But all the extra costs that you aren't considering get expensive.

Financing is often another huge factor in purchasing a car. Many people finance, but if you're able to save up the money first, it saves thousands of dollars to pay in full. Financing a car for six years at 5 percent APR (annual interest paid) is over $2,000 in interest on a $15,000 vehicle over the life of the loan with 10 percent down. If you saved up first and then purchased a vehicle in cash, you save yourself thousands of dollars.

So often we think that we need to finance a car. But if you flip your mind-set, you can pay yourself instead of the dealer. Who doesn't want to do that? You then make over $1,000 every three years! Fourteen percent of the total cost is interest, not 5 percent! For doing nothing. Don't give that money away.

YEAR	BEGINNING BALANCE	INTEREST	PRINCIPAL	ENDING BALANCE
1	13,500.00	630.06	1,978.98	11,521.06
2	11,521.06	528.80	2,080.24	9,440.87
3	9,440.87	422.39	2,186.65	7,254.26
4	7,254.26	310.53	2,298.51	4,955.77
5	4,955.77	192.93	2,416.11	2,539.69
6	2,539.69	69.31	2,539.73	0

If you do decide that financing is your only option, you rarely want to finance through the dealer. Often you'll see a 0.0% financing deal on television and think that it will apply to you. It probably won't. It will likely only apply to a new vehicle purchased by people with perfect credit. This is another trick they use to sucker you in and get you on the lot. What you want to do is not finance at all, but if you must, get four different places to offer you an interest rate. I recommend asking the dealer and three banks. You can approach the banks prior to buying a vehicle, give them the basic information regarding the kind of vehicle you want to purchase, and be pre-approved for a loan.

Shop around at different banks in the area. Normally, the smaller the better. They will give you a rate based on the car, the price, and the length of the note. You want the best deal possible.

GET A REAL DEAL—YOUR WAY

Now that you know a little bit about the numbers and how they work, it's important to know how to leverage your position in the relationship to create the best deal. With a car salesman, it is rare you will work with them again. You don't need a best friend. By the end of the time together, you want them to be tired of you. You want to push, push, and push some more.

Here are additional tips for purchasing a car:

- Never buy a car when you absolutely must have it (a.k.a. you're walking to work). Always be in the position where they (the car dealer) need you, you don't need them.
- Always buy at the end of the month or at the end of the year. Every dealer has a quota they need to hit. You're helping them, not the other way around.
- Always walk away from the car at least once (even if you're sure you'll buy it). I walked away from my current vehicle (a Toyota Tundra) four times before finally purchasing it.
- Always know what you want and your total walk-away price (not the monthly cost). Know this number *before* looking at cars and stick to it.

- Never lease a car. Ever. Ever. You have no equity in the vehicle. You are always paying someone for a car. Forever. It just doesn't make sense unless your company is paying for your car. A lease is a dangerous thing because there are mileage restrictions and a host of other issues that keep you locked to that vehicle for better or worse.

- Never buy a new car. Always buy a used car. The moment you drive the vehicle off the lot, it's immediately worth thousands less, up to half the car's value (average is about 30 percent). The average new car loses $15,000 in value in just five years. I prefer a vehicle that is one or two years old; that way, someone else has already taken the depreciation hit (*depreciation* is the term used for an asset losing its value over time).

- Decide on the car, year, and price you are willing to spend. Then email all the dealers within fifty miles and give them the make, model, and year. Have them bid on your business. Remember, they need you; you don't need them.

- If you visit a high-volume dealer, they make their money on how many cars they move and get an incentive from their corporation. When we purchased my wife's vehicle, I asked for the invoice they paid for the car. I saw the amount they paid and then paid them that amount. Technically, they didn't make anything off us. But they made incentive money from Toyota because of the volume of cars they move.

- Pay for use of a website that gives you more data on what to pay for a car. Consumer Reports and Kelly Blue Book are great.

- If you're looking for a solid, long-term-use sedan, go with a Honda or Toyota. They will last forever if you take care of them (and repairs are less expensive).

- Low mileage is more important than a newer year if you will be in the car for a long time.

- This is a large purchase that has the potential to impact your credit for a long time. If you decide to finance, remember that the appeal of the vehicle in month one will not be true five years later when you are still paying for that vehicle. When that car has dents, scratches, and a cracked windshield, you're still paying just as much in month sixty as you are in month one. So beware.

OTHER BUYING TIPS—NOT FROM A DEALER

1. Get familiar with all the different buying options. There are so many platforms to search. Craigslist, cars.com, Carmax, dealers that sell trade-ins, and many more.
2. Post on social media the specific car you're looking for. Who knows, you might get lucky with a connection.
3. When you contact a seller, have some questions ready that would be deal-breakers for you. Examples of these can be:
    + How many owners has the car had?
    + Do you have any maintenance records?
    + Is there anything else about this car that I should know? Potential problems?
    + Is the price negotiable? (All prices are negotiable.)
4. Want to make sure you're getting a good deal? Check out these websites: Edmunds.com, KBB.com, NADA.com, or CarGurus.com for the true market value, which may vary with where you live in the country.
5. Get accident and safety reports. If you want to proceed, get the VIN (vehicle identification number), which is a seventeen-digit code inside the front dash at the base of the windshield and also on a sticker on the driver's side door edge where it latches. Then order a CARFAX report and check the car's recall history by visiting the National Highway Traffic Safety Administration's website.
6. If everything checks out, take it for a test drive and have a trustworthy independent mechanic do a used-car check. Usually it's $50 or $100, but it's well worth it. If a seller won't allow this, run away from the deal.

7. If it all looks good, negotiate a price and then write up a two-sentence contract that says what you are paying for the car (called a bill of sale).

Buying a car is a fun, exciting time. It's even better when you get an amazing deal that you're proud of.

THE BIG 3

- Take a deep breath and don't be overwhelmed when buying a vehicle.
- There will always be another deal.
- Always take your car to a mechanic to have it inspected before purchasing.

#GETANAPARTMENT

Now that we have established that with a large purchase comes many hidden costs, it's now time to dive into the question of "Where should I live?"

First, you have to figure out where you are in life. Are you moving to an area for a long period of time or will you be moving again in just a couple of years? In order to warrant buying versus renting, you need to commit to stay there for at least five years. If you spend less than five years in an area, then you should rent.

The five-year marker is simply a filter and not a hard and fast rule. The reason for that length is because most of your first five years paying into a mortgage is just interest and very little principal, so you don't own much of your home after five years. And when you go to sell, you have to pay a real estate agent, closing costs, and even the other person's real estate agent.

HOME-BUYING TERMS

Before we go too far down the idea of home buying, let's outline some terms that you'll hear but might have no idea what they mean:

- *Conventional loan*: A mortgage that follows a set of loan guidelines. This is the most common, and most likely what you will use. Other potential loans are nonconforming, government, jumbo, and subprime.
- *APR (annual percentage rate):* The cost of credit on a yearly basis expressed as a percentage. This rate includes certain costs paid to obtain the loan and is usually higher than the

interest rate. This helps you understand the bigger picture of what a loan will actually cost.

- *PMI (private mortgage insurance)*: An extra monthly fee on top of your regular mortgage payment if you make a down payment of less than 20 percent of the home's equity. In addition to owning less of your home, you'll have to pay even more money each month for your payment until you get to the 20 percent equity mark. This insurance is in the event that you default (stop paying) on your loan. The insurance kicks in and helps to protect the lender. Don't be confused. Defaulting still kills your credit score and makes it much harder for you to borrow in the future.

- *DTI (debt-to-income ratio)*: How much money you owe on long-term debt divided by your gross (pre-tax) monthly income. The normal rule of thumb is to not spend more than 25 percent of your gross income on housing (mortgage, insurance, taxes, etc.). I (Josh) would argue that even 25 percent is too high. So if you make $48,000 at your first job out of college, you need to be all in at $1,000 per month (or less) for your rent or mortgage payment. If it is higher than this percentage, you should get a roommate.

- *Closing*: When a real estate transaction is finalized and all parties receive what they are due. The buyer gets a home and the seller gets money for the property. This is not free though. The expenses associated with closing on a house are not small. You have to pay assorted fees you probably didn't know existed. And remember, as with nearly everything in life, this is negotiable. When I bought my home, I called up several title companies and shopped around. They all provide a similar service. I was looking for the cheapest one.

- *Settlement*: A reconciliation of the accounts that takes place as a part of closing. You receive a document that shows you where all the money is going.

- *Escrow*: An account that holds funds for future payment. For someone with a mortgage, you should escrow your taxes and insurance payments. Every month you owe money for the mortgage, but you only pay insurance and taxes once a year (although most people choose to pay the money they will owe for both of these items each month instead of in one lump sum). You have to pay insurance in advance for the year, and you pay taxes after the year is over.

SHOULD I BUY A HOUSE?

Now that we got those terms out of the way, it's important to understand where the money in that mortgage payment goes each month. Once you understand mortgage payments (and home amortization), then you'll understand why you shouldn't move before living in a house for five years. Why? The reason behind this is connected to the expense of closing on a house and how very little of your money actually goes to earning equity on the home during the first few years.

Equity is the amount of the house that you own. You may think that if you pay a $1,000 mortgage payment, that $1,000 of that payment goes toward you owning the home—and that the amount you owe on your house will go down by $1,000. Nope.

Right after you buy your house, most of that payment goes toward interest and only a little goes toward principal. Every month you pay interest on the amount of the house that you still owe. The quicker you pay down the principal (balance of the mortgage), the less interest you pay over the life of the loan. Now let's take a look at a home mortgage of $150,000 for thirty years at 4.5 percent interest:

MONTH	PAYMENT	PRINCIPAL	INTEREST	TOTAL INTEREST	BALANCE REMAINING
1	760	198	562	562	149,802
2	760	198	562	1,124	149,604
3	760	199	561	1,685	149,405

MONTH	PAYMENT	PRINCIPAL	INTEREST	TOTAL INTEREST	BALANCE REMAINING
4	760	200	560	2,245	149,205
5	760	201	559	2,804	149,004
6	760	201	559	3,363	148,803
7	760	202	558	3,921	148,601
8	760	203	557	4,478	148,398
9	760	204	556	5,034	148,194
10	760	204	556	5,590	147,990
11	760	205	555	6,145	147,785
12	760	206	554	6,699	147,579
Total	**9,120**	**2,421**	**6,699**	**6,699**	**147,579**

After the first year of home ownership, in addition to paying closing costs, paying real estate agents, buying furniture, etc., you have paid over $9,000 toward your home. That's exciting. You are making progress. But of that $9,000 you spent, only $2,421 went toward the principal of the home. That's a ton of work for very little return. This is why if you're living somewhere for only a few years, home ownership probably doesn't make sense. Below is the chart mapping out the first five years:

YEAR	TOTAL PAYMENTS	PRINCIPAL PAID	INTEREST PAID	ENDING PRINCIPAL BALANCE
1	9,120	2,421	6,699	147,579
2	9,120	2,531	6,589	145,048
3	9,120	2,647	6,473	142,401
4	9,120	2,769	6,351	139,632
5	9,120	2,896	6,224	136,736

What are some other factors that you may not be considering when you look at a home on Zillow? There are a number of additional expenses that drive up the monthly cost of your home including:

- Mortgage insurance (if you don't make at least a 20 percent down payment on a home)
- Home insurance
- Taxes
- Repairs and maintenance

Home insurance and taxes will vary tremendously based upon the area of the country where you live. All this information is to help prepare you for the unexpected. Don't get too anxious or excited. Be patient until you can make a wise financial decision.

If you decide to go the home route, I highly recommend saving so you'll have a strong (20%) down payment and avoid the additional mortgage insurance. (I hate giving my money to other people for an unnecessary service.) Here are a few other pitfalls that you will want to avoid:

- Check your credit *before* you start house shopping. If you find the home of your dreams and then get the ball rolling on paperwork, you're way too late. You need to have your credit score in order because this is that time when you finally need to leverage your great score. It makes a difference of tens of thousands of dollars over the course of the loan.
- Don't apply for other credit during the time of house shopping. Credit scores are a really tricky beast (more about that later in the book). They're impacted by how much you have available to spend as well as the length of time you've had accounts. If you suddenly start opening or closing credit accounts, it will throw everything off. Give yourself six months to a year prior to buying a home to make sure that your credit is in order. Last-moment excitement over a new credit card could cost you for many years to come.
- As you're beginning to look at homes, go ahead and talk to a bank (preferably several) and get the ball rolling on pre-qualification. Don't wait until you need the money, because this

is not a fast or simple process. It's best if you go into home buying knowing exactly what you can afford and what the interest rates will be. Don't find your dream home and then try to secure financing.

APARTMENT HUNTING

You say home ownership isn't for you yet. That's great, so you decide to rent. Perhaps you plan on being in an area for only a couple of years. Perhaps you don't know the area and don't want to buy a home in the wrong part of town.

When I moved to Little Rock, my wife and I planned on it being a two- to three-year move. In addition to that, we had no idea about the city or where we wanted to live. So we found an apartment complex and planned on staying there until we decided where we would be long term. Here are some major considerations while seeking an apartment:

- Is it safe? What kind of area is it in?
- Read the entire lease. Often, leasing agents will hide a bunch of different fees inside the lease in the event you have to move out early. For instance, you may owe several months' rent and you forfeit your security deposit (I know this from my own experience).
- Where is the apartment located? Ask other people you know from that town where they live or where they would recommend.
- What is the traffic situation like?
- Are utilities included? What about cable?

Apartment living or house renting is great for a time and makes sense if you're early in your career and saving up or if you're trying to decide where you'd like to live. Don't feel the pressure to catch up to other friends. You have a long time to earn more money and move into a home. Remember, the more rooms you have, the more furniture and decor you need to fill them. And furniture is not cheap.

Large purchases are exciting and a lot of fun if you're able to go into them wisely. Never go in blind. Have a plan. Ask advice from someone who has made the same purchase recently. Make sure that you're maximizing your hard-earned money. Salespeople and banks are not on your side when it comes to purchasing cars and homes. You need to be extremely knowledgeable about the decisions that have the possibility to impact you for the next thirty years.

THE BIG 3

- Don't be a sucker. Know your numbers before you make a big purchase.
- With homes, the true price is much higher than the sale price.
- Apartments are a great decision for young adults.

#ADULTSNEEDINSURANCE

Suddenly, you're considered an adult. Responsible for everything. You need to pay your own bills, find your own place to live, go to work on time, and perhaps even try to plan for the future. You've always known about car insurance. Not because you understood it but because if you didn't have it, you couldn't drive. Maybe you understood your insurance policy or maybe you didn't.

There are two ways to view the money that you have for "saving." Some products you purchase exist to protect what you own (insurance) while others are designed to help you build additional wealth (investments such as mutual funds, stocks, bonds, etc.). Let me (Josh) tell you why you can't live without insurance and why failing to have it could be catastrophic.

Insurance is the most effective way to make sure you and your family (or future family) are safe—from the effects of a fire, car accident, sickness, and even death. There is an insurance policy for each of them. As an adult, you need insurance. Not having it exposes you to liability (things that you are responsible for) that could ruin you before you even get started.

You'll hear about a million kinds of insurance, and I'm sure you have many questions: *How does it all work? What do I really need? Who do I talk to? How do I know which is the cheapest? Is the cheapest the best?* Let's dive into the most important type of insurance first.

HEALTH INSURANCE

This is rapidly becoming more and more expensive while offering less and less coverage. Due to recent changes in health care policy, you are now able to stay on your parents' insurance until you are twenty-six. If you are able, ride this out. It will be way cheaper to stay with them than to split and pay it on your own. Once you're nearing twenty-six, you'll want to find coverage. It will likely be through your employer.

If your employer doesn't offer affordable health insurance for you, then you may be eligible to receive subsidies (up to a certain income level) through your state's health insurance marketplace. Every state has this available. Just go to Google and type in "[the state that you live in]'s health insurance exchange." This has been an issue with a lot of emotion (and expense) behind it for many years, and while this information could rapidly change, the fact is that you always need health insurance. If you don't have insurance and something catastrophic happens, you could never fully recover from the expense of the hospital bills.

Currently, if you don't have health insurance, you're subject to a penalty on your annual taxes (there are some exceptions). And you absolutely want to have health insurance even if you're young and healthy. A freak accident may land you in the hospital, and you want to be able to pay for this service and not go into major debt.

While shopping for health insurance, you'll hear the terms *deductible* and *premium*. What do these terms mean? The deductible is the amount that you pay *before* insurance kicks in. For example, if you have a $1,000 deductible, your insurance company doesn't begin paying anything until you've paid $1,000 out of pocket for that year. Then you may have coinsurance, which means that you pay a portion and they pay a portion, until you reach your annual spending limit. The premium is how much you pay monthly for the insurance.

If you're young and healthy, look at a lower-premium, higher-deductible plan. That way you don't unnecessarily pay for a service you will (hopefully) rarely use. If you have a personal or family history of certain illnesses, then you'll want a plan with a deductible that is lower so that insurance will begin paying faster. This plan will involve a higher premium.

CAR INSURANCE

Slightly less morbid but no less important is the need for car insurance. This is critical to your ability to get from point A to point B. Without car insurance, you're unable to legally drive. But even something as simple as car insurance can be highly complex, so we'll simplify this the best we can. There are two primary kinds of car insurance.

Let's start with the first and most basic kind of insurance, liability. This is the minimum policy required to drive. Liability insurance provides financial help for the *other* driver(s) in the event you get into an accident and it's *your* fault. It covers their car repair expenses and medical bills (it doesn't provide anything for you, though). If you total your car, you're out of luck. This is similar to a cheese pizza. It's the most basic combination of ingredients you can possibly have and still call the circular piece of cheesy bread a pizza.

If you fail to have any kind of car insurance at all, you'll go hungry. Something will happen to you and your car. It is not a matter of if but when.

I have a friend, Susie, who spent all her money buying a car and forgot to save any of it for the monthly insurance cost. She had just purchased a new car and loved showing it off. Susie knew she needed insurance to purchase her vehicle , so she bought insurance and brought her license and proof of insurance when she bought the car. Upon leaving the dealership, Susie decided that she really didn't need this expensive insurance that she was paying; especially since she was trying to pay off the car quickly. She had about $11,000 remaining on the balance of the vehicle, and that extra $100 per month she was spending on insurance would really help. Besides, she had always been a good driver and didn't really worry about accidents.

A couple of months after calling her insurance agent and canceling her insurance, she was involved in an accident that was her fault. (Remember, don't text and drive.) She still owed almost $11,000 on the car. Not only did she have to pay several thousand dollars in damages to the other car, but she also had to pay the remaining $11,000 on her car—which was now totaled (repairs would cost more than the value of the car) and not drivable. If you ever want to be furious, try paying for a car that you no longer have. Now try paying for that car for several more years. But a hundred dollars per month could have saved her all that money and frustration.

The crazy part is that it could have been so much worse. What if Susie had gotten into that accident without insurance and someone got hurt—or even worse, died? What if Susie was expected to pay for all the medical bills, funeral expenses, and lawsuit expenses for the family of the person in the accident? Susie was only eighteen years old. This accident could have ruined her financial life for the foreseeable future.

Now that you're depressed and scared about ever driving again, let's talk about the supreme pizza. This is the top-of-the-line insurance (and generally not much more expensive than liability); it's called full coverage auto insurance.

Full coverage is exactly what it sounds like (and what Susie needed). In the event you get into an accident and it is *your* fault, *both* cars are covered. This policy is required if you drive a car that has not been paid off. Once you own the car outright, you can carry only liability insurance. Still, full coverage is the best way to sleep well at night. It provides a tremendous comfort to know that if something happens while driving, you and those around you will be financially safe. The worst thing that could happen would be to get into a wreck that is your fault and then be sued by the other person for medical bills. You will be sued for money that you don't have because you didn't carry insurance. Then you could owe thousands of dollars before even starting your career.

So how do you decide which type of insurance to carry? If you own an old beater that's worth only a few thousand dollars, you definitely want to carry only liability insurance because the additional cost associated with full coverage is too great for repairing a car with little worth. If you drive a car that is either not paid for or worth more than $5,000, I would highly suggest full coverage. This allows you to repair the car much more easily and keep driving longer.

So do you have to pay anything when you have an accident? Yes, similar to health insurance, you have a deductible that applies anytime you get work done through insurance. This deductible can be high or low; it's up to you. Once you've met that deductible, the car insurance company covers the rest (this is slightly different than with health insurance).

The reason the deductible is in place is to avoid fraud for the insurance companies. When you select your insurance coverage, you have to pick your premium (which you pay monthly, quarterly, or annually). The lower the premium , the higher the deductible (same as health insurance). Essentially, the less you pay up front (monthly), the more you pay in the event that something happens (deductible). Or you could go the other way. You could have a higher monthly payment but know that you won't have to pay as much out of pocket when an accident occurs. These rates are entirely dependent upon age, driving history, type of vehicle, and other variables.

Riders

Riders are not the people in the car with you but rather additions onto the policy that you select. This applies to your liability policy. If you have the cheese pizza option, then I recommend adding a couple of toppings just to keep you safe. Most riders are baked in to the cost of the full coverage so you don't have to worry about these (but still ask your insurance agent to confirm).

You can have just about anything under the sun added to your policy, but the one I recommend the most is uninsured motorists insurance. Yes, even though it is illegal, there are still plenty of people on the road without insurance. In the instance that you get hit by someone who doesn't have insurance and they leave the scene, you're stuck holding the bill (unless you can find them and sue). Even if you sue, most of the folks who don't carry insurance don't have anything that would be worth suing for. That's a pretty bad place to be in. Pay the extra couple of dollars each month to cover yourself.

RENTER AND HOME OWNER'S INSURANCE

Now that you've found yourself the right car insurance policy, it's time to locate a policy to cover the place where you live. If you're renting an apartment or house, you want renter's insurance, and if you're purchasing a home, you need (and are required to have) homeowner's insurance.

Renter's insurance is a great insurance to have to protect your valuables in the event of an emergency at your residence (a fire, flood, etc.). This is especially valuable in an apartment complex where your neighbors could do something that could end up impacting you. Renter's insurance is inexpensive, and if combined with an auto policy, you can receive a discount. The more policies you have to your name, the more multi-line discounts you can receive.

Renter's insurance works similar to car insurance in that if something were to happen, you pay a deductible and then can collect the check for valuables lost over and above that amount. It also works for individual items that you insure. If your home gets broken into and someone steals your TV and laptop, they would be covered.

Whenever you sign up for this policy, make sure to take pictures of the most valuable items in your possession, as well as general images of your home or apartment. It's much easier, when filing a claim, if you can prove through receipts or photos that you had the property to begin with. If you have renter's insurance with a company and then purchase a home, you get additional discounts for already being a member. Make sure to always have coverage on your residence in the event of an emergency.

A young man named James had a horrible situation take place not too long ago. James is a remarkable young man but had unfortunately just lost his job. He and his wife were working hard to make ends meet. The same week that he lost his job, his next-door neighbor had a terrible fire. Tragically, the woman in the apartment passed away. James and his wife severely impacted by this unfortunate event. Their apartment filled with smoke and they had to evacuate. It ruined their TV, clothes, computer, and furniture. This story would have been tragic for James if he and his wife hadn't had insurance. They would've been responsible for replacing everything even though it was someone else's fault—a nearly devastating blow.

But James had insurance. Renter's insurance swooped in and took care of him and his wife. Their insurance helped them replace everything they had lost. They were able to prove what they had lost, paid their deductible, and were able to move on with life.

LIFE INSURANCE

Now that you have your car and home covered, it would be valuable to look into a life insurance policy. Life insurance has its proponents and opponents. I'm simply providing one perspective.

Life insurance is basically death insurance. It only kicks in when you die. Kind of a bummer to discuss, but it's an important subject. If you're fresh out of school and heading into the workforce, life insurance isn't a big deal. The numbers show that your likelihood of dying is minimal, so I wouldn't recommend this coverage yet. I'm a firm believer in the value of life insurance, but not until you're providing for a family or have a bill that will outlive you (like a mortgage).

Think of life insurance as income replacement. If you die with no spouse or children and no debt, then your income doesn't need to be replaced. Life insurance becomes significantly more critical when you get married, have a child, or purchase a home. If none of this has happened yet, then feel free to jump to the next chapter. Life insurance is not recommended until you have something or someone to provide for after your death.

Before diving into how much coverage you need, let's talk about the different types of life insurance that exist.

Term Life

Term life is the most common and least expensive. This is the avenue that I would recommend for most young people. You get the most for your money through this method. As the name reflects, it's only for a set time. You can have term insurance for one year or up to around thirty years. The longer the term, the more expensive the policy. This is because with every year that passes, the more likely you are to die (sorry to bum you out). A ten-year policy will be much less expensive than a thirty-year policy. Also, you want a "level term" policy, meaning that you pay the same amount in the last year that you paid in the first year of coverage. The other option is a policy that is cheap up front but gets more expensive as you get older. This isn't what you want.

Whole Life

Whole life is the most expensive. This product gives you coverage for the entirety of your life and never expires as long as you pay your premiums. When you die, your family gets this money. The downside to this is the expense associated with it. You'll earn more money by taking the difference between the cost of term insurance and the cost of whole insurance and investing it in mutual funds (which we will talked about earlier).

These are two of the most common available products to insure against your death. Now we'll discuss the amount of money you'll want those policies to insure for.

Life Insurance Coverage

There are two main reasons you want to have life insurance—so money will be there for:

1. Outstanding debts such as a mortgage, private student loans (federal student loans are canceled upon death), credit card debt, etc. You want your life insurance to be greater than these items combined because if you don't, you'll send those bills (from the grave) to your loved ones. You don't want to burden them with your problems after passing on.
2. Family income for your spouse and dependents. Use a 10x multiplier to determine your family income needs. What that means is if you're making $50,000 at your job, then you'll want $500,000

above the total of your debts. This will give your spouse about a ten-year income cushion in order to land properly on his or her feet.

We have talked about how much insurance you need. Now the question is for how long do you need it.

Having life insurance is most critical when you begin having children. You want to provide sufficient insurance to see them through their educational years (including college). Make sure to leave enough money to see them sufficiently into adulthood. I recommend a long policy (twenty years or more) so you have enough coverage to at least see your children get out of the home.

PERSONAL ARTICLES LIABILITY POLICY

This is insurance for an individual large-ticket item such as an engagement ring. You would purchase a separate policy (or a rider on your home owner's policy) to cover the expense of a valuable diamond ring. This protects you in the event that the ring is lost or stolen. It's also only about 1 percent of the cost of the item per year. Unless you own a very high-dollar item, this policy isn't for you.

HOW TO FIND INSURANCE

Health insurance is provided on a state level. UnitedHealth Care is a big player as is Blue Cross Blue Shield. Google the health insurance providers in your state and price them out on the exchanges available if your employer does not offer this benefit.

Car, home, renter, personal article, and every other kind of insurance can be found a number of different ways. The biggest players in the auto industry are State Farm, Berkshire Hathaway, Allstate, and Progressive. You can seek these companies out directly, or you can look for a local insurance broker that can underwrite (give you coverage) for numerous companies. If you have more than one policy with the same company, they generally offer you discounts. Try to bundle policies when possible for the best savings.

THE BIG 3

- Get health and car insurance to protect your future finances.
- Get renter's/home owner's insurance to protect all of your possessions.
- Get life insurance once you get married, have a child, or buy a home.

15

#INEEDCREDIT

	Amount Owed by Average U.S. Household with this Type of Debt	Total Debt Owed by U.S. Consumers
Credit Cards	$16,883	$784 Billion
Mortgages	$182,421	$8.69 Trillion
Auto Loans	$29,539	$1.19 Trillion
Student Loans	$50,626	$1.34 Trillion
Any Type of Debt	$137,063	$12.84 Trillion

These numbers are from the Federal Reserve Q2 2017.[1]

"**B**ut I need to build my credit!" I (Josh) am told this by nearly every young person I've talked to about credit. It's also one of the most dangerous phrases out there unless you understand what credit is and how to use it.

Great credit is liberating and can provide you with the best rates for car insurance, buying a house, and even landing a job. Bad credit is a heavy weight dragging you down that you can't escape. It results in terrible rates when you're looking for any kind of financing (which causes you to spend more money on the same item, further perpetuating the cycle).

Finances are one of the leading causes of divorce in America. A large part of this is due to debt and bad credit. One of my dear friends, John, is one of the hardest working people I know. He met his lovely wife named Ann. She was perfect for him in so many ways. They dated and finally decided to get married.

After the wedding, my buddy John discovered she had a dark secret: she had a lot of consumer (credit card) debt. She had racked it up at a young age buying impulse items that she didn't need. As a student, she never earned enough money to be able to be able to pay it back. She found herself on the merry-go-round of endless interest payments. Ann made this mistake in her youthful excitement, and it was still haunting her into her marriage.

She never wanted that baggage to be seen, but it was eating at her. John entered the marriage and now one person's bad credit was suddenly the concern of two. Even if you're the one with bad debt, it impacts your spouse. If you both need to sign for a loan or finance anything, the creditors will look at both of your scores. It impacted John and Ann whenever they went to look at apartments or buy a vehicle. Her credit score was so low that her costs for any financing skyrocketed.

So how do you avoid this?

It is important to understand exactly how credit works.

You have a credit score. Actually, you have three. Three different companies monitor you, and even one of these companies that may have bad information can cost you the better interest rate or price. These companies exist to share with future creditors your credit history. You need to make sure the information they have is right.

The three major monitoring companies are Experian, Equifax and TransUnion.

What goes into your credit score? How is it determined?

- Payment history (35 percent). Have you always paid your bill on time? Did you ever miss a payment?
- Amount owed (30 percent). You should be using less than 35 percent of the amount that you have available. For example, if you have a $10,000 credit line, you should never have more than $3,500 spent.
- Length of credit history (15 percent). It's important to have a few credit lines with a long history compared to a bunch of lines that are new. Five years or more is ideal.

- New credit (10 percent). If you open new credit lines, it can hurt your score. Not only does it show the creditors that you're looking for more debt, but it also shortens the life on your overall credit history.
- Types of credit used (10 percent). Is your credit a mortgage, student loans, a car loan, or credit cards?

So what would be a good score?

A credit score ranges from 300 to 850. A credit score below 700 is poor. A score of 700 to 800 is good. Anything above 800 is considered excellent. Most credit scores fall between 600 and 750, but millennial scores average around 625. No wonder it's so expensive to get a loan from a bank! Only half of millennials have even checked their credit score.

Stats also show that about 20 percent of credit reports have incorrect data that could be harming your score. If you have any legitimate bad marks against your account, it takes seven years to get them off. Credit agencies want to see improvement for a long time before they allow delinquent marks to roll off.

So what can you do to set yourself up for success building credit? Here are some little tricks to help you crank up that credit score:

1. Check your score. Tons of places online will do this for you for free. Credit Karma is one site where you can take a look. The first step is knowing where you're starting from.
2. *Always* pay on time. This is the biggest part of your score. If you mess this up, you'll be regretting it for the next seven years. Even if you can't pay the full amount, you have to pay the minimum. Do not get behind on this.
3. Don't run high balances on your credit cards, even if you pay on time. Don't charge a high percentage of your available credit. This can negatively impact your score. Try to stay around the 10 to 15 percent range. For example, if you have a credit card that has a $10,000 limit, don't charge more than $1,000 to $1,500 total.

4. Don't open a bunch of credit cards at once. This can negatively impact your score if you suddenly have a bunch of new lines.

5. Hang on to your lines of credit for a while. Even if you don't use the card, as long as you aren't paying an annual fee, it's best to cut up the card and throw it away (and leave it open) than to close the account.

6. If you have parents you trust, ask them to make you an additional card member but to not give you the card. This way your name is tied to the account that shows usage and consistent payments. This helps to build your credit history. But the reverse could also be true. If your parents aren't great at money management, don't ask them to do this.

In order to be a truly savvy user of credit, it is critical to understand how the other side works. How does the credit card company make money?

- Most of the money earned is through the interest payments of people carrying a balance each month. This is how credit card companies exist. Don't be a sucker by giving them your money for doing nothing.

- There are annual fees for some cards, cash advance fees, balance transfer fees, and late fees. One of the best sites out there to assess different credit cards and learn some tricks is nerdwallet.com.

- Interchange: This is where the company charges the merchant 1 to 3 percent of the transaction total for allowing the use of their card as payment.

It's also vital to understand what APR means and how it impacts you. APR stands for annual percentage rate. This is different from an interest rate. At its simplest, the interest rate reflects the current cost of borrowing. The APR provides a more complete picture by taking the interest rate as a starting point and accounting for lender fees required to finance the loan.

What's a normal APR? Over 15 percent.

We mentioned that the interest payments are what keeps the credit companies in business. How exactly does that work? Here's an example: Say you really, really want that new television for the Super Bowl. The 75" LED TV is on sale right now on Amazon for $2,000. You don't have the money at the moment, but that's all right. You're expecting your tax refund to come back any day now, and you'll get the money from that. Not a problem.

So you go ahead and get the new TV. And it's beautiful. You have all your buddies come out for the big game and showcase the most impressive screen to all your friends. A couple of weeks later, you get a letter from the IRS stating that you incorrectly filled out your taxes and that you aren't due a refund. You don't owe any money, but you aren't getting anything back. Especially $2,000 for a new television.

Now what do you do? You don't have that money, and you can't return the TV. You look at the credit card statement that comes in. No worries. The statement says that you only owe $60. That isn't bad at all. You can pay $60. And in no time, it'll be paid off, right?

Wrong! If the interest rate is 18 percent (a common rate) and you only pay the minimum payment of 3 percent (or $60), it will take you eleven years and six months to pay off that television. Do you still think that TV will be awesome almost twelve years from now? Probably not. In addition, you will also have paid nearly $1,700 in interest—that makes the TV almost twice as expensive as you originally thought. Not such a great idea anymore.

Often, the immediate gratification of wanting something overrides our ability to wait for the right thing. Many people use credit as an avenue for immediate gratification. They want something now, and they will pay for it later. This is a mind-set that will cost you much more in the long run. It's how poor people think about money.

How do you avoid this kind of situation? Make sure you understand how credit works and how you can use it to your advantage. Make credit work for you, not the other way around. Once you are enslaved to a bad score or a minimum credit card payment, it can feel as if there's no way out. Don't let that happen.

The easiest way is to avoid credit cards in general: use your bank's debit card after college while you're just getting started. Having a credit card makes the temptation too great. The reward is not worth the risk!

THE BIG 3

→ Credit cards are tempting. Use a bank (debit) card instead.

→ Know your credit score and how it is calculated.

→ Never buy something you don't have the money for.

PART 6

TIME
MANAGEMENT

16

#BIGROCKS

Have you ever set out to accomplish an important task and before you know it, you've been watching YouTube videos of Michael Jackson impersonators doing magic tricks for four hours? Yeah, me neither. Asking for a friend. For most of us, probably not you though, accomplishing the most important tasks can be a challenge.

I (Pete) had a friend who was in charge of a large business with hundreds of employees. Let's call her Courtney. She always seemed to have time to do the things she wanted to do. I asked her how she was able to achieve this. She told me there are a few questions she asks herself at the beginning of every day:

1. What is the most important thing I have to do today?
2. What are the things that only I can do?
3. Can anyone else do anything on my to-do list 80 percent as well as I can? (If the answer to that question was yes, she delegated it to them.)

TIME MANAGEMENT

How do you manage your time? First of all, the language about time is misleading. Everyone has the same amount of time. The president of the United States, babies, CEOs, entry-level interns, students, etc. all have the same 24 hours per day (168 hours per week). You can't buy more, and you can't wish for more (well, you can try, but it won't work). We all need to make the most of what we're given.

Think about the last time you said, "I just don't have the time." We all say it (or think it), but it's not true. We do have the time. We've just chosen to use our time in other ways.

You have exactly enough time to do what you're supposed to do today. This chapter will help you seize your time and take action. Don't prioritize your schedule; schedule your priorities.

HOW TO MAXIMIZE YOUR TIME, ACCOMPLISH MORE, AND DO THE RIGHT THINGS

1. Prioritize. Put the big rocks in first.
   + Ask yourself, *What's the most important thing I should do today?* Then go after it with everything you have. Right away.
   + Start big tasks with the first step. Don't put *Do project* on your to-do list; use *Start project*. Sometimes just a tweak as seemingly small as that can make a big difference.

2. Have you ever noticed that your work is like a liquid? It expands or contracts according to the time allotted for it? Cut back on the hours given to a project or task to increase overall efficiency. Tim Ferriss has some great things to say about this in his book *The 4-Hour Work Week*. It's worth a look if you've never read it.
   + Meetings should always have an end time. When they do, it forces the participants to get done what they need to get done in the time allotted.
   + Prioritizing is like a muscle. When you first start, it's awkward and feels uncomfortable and sore. But when you begin to figure out what's important, you exercise it every day and decisions are more easily made because you know your priorities.

3. You need a headquarters. This is somewhere that you write *everything* down. It's your hub. Doesn't matter if it's on paper or in your phone or on stone tablets, but you need somewhere that you keep every task, project, appointment, note, idea, etc. I love using Evernote and the notes section of my iPhone; they are my digital brain.

4. Have a regular set planning time for your week. Maybe Sunday night. Maybe Monday morning *before* you go in to work. Plan out each day in the morning. Ten minutes of planning saves an hour of time. It gives purpose and direction for your day.

5. Be early, everywhere! This will show your coworkers and employees that you take yourself seriously, and you take their time seriously. Also, you won't be in a hurry. Something that can help you do this well is not trying to fit that one last thing in before leaving. This is a killer for me. I'm always trying to squeeze out one more drop of a task or another call or that last email. If you get in the habit of getting up early, then life is much calmer.

6. Always have a book/Kindle/etc. with you everywhere you go. Just last week I arrived five minutes early to a lunch meeting. As I sat down, I got a text that my friend would be about twenty minutes late. That's almost a half hour. So seize the time. Make it your own.

7. If something takes less than three minutes, do it immediately (unless you're running late). I like to build momentum with a couple small wins. Then tackle the most important thing of the day.

8. Delegate when appropriate. If someone can do a job or task 80 percent as well as you, have them do it.

9. Minimum effective dose. Find out what it will take to get it done. Don't sacrifice on excellence, but making something 10 percent better usually requires 100 percent more effort. Make sure it'll be worth it if you're going to expend this extra effort.

10. Have chunks of the day when you put your phone on airplane mode (of course, check with your boss and make sure this is okay). I promise these will be the most productive hours of your day. You need uninterrupted time every day.

11. Put everything into your schedule. Are you a spiritual person? Put time in for prayer/meditation. Are you exercising? Put it

in your schedule. What matters to you? Put the "big rocks" in first and guard them with your life. First things first. Then when someone asks you to do something, you can reply honestly "I'm sorry, but I already have a commitment." The more organized you are, the more spontaneous you can be.

PUT THE BIG ROCKS IN FIRST

You probably haven't had to prioritize too much so far in life. You could handle everything as it came to you. But this is real life. Now you have to figure out what is most important. And often these decisions cross over different arenas in your life. Is it more important to call your brother back or to finish that spreadsheet for your boss? Is it more important to go to your friend's art show opening or go home for the weekend and see your niece's recital?

How will you make these decisions? You need to prioritize.

You must put the big rocks into the jar first if they are to fit. You must decide what's important to you and make sure your best time goes there. That's why your calendar is your best friend. You can look out for an entire year (or at least a semester) and decide what is most important to you. Family? Write in some family visit time. Block off a couple weekends. Friends? Significant other? Travel? If you don't schedule your time, someone else will.

You're in control of your time. Don't let other people prioritize it for you. Just remember that every yes is a no to something else.

Entrepreneur Derek Sivers has a litmus test for when he's presented with options or a request to speak or be involved in a new venture. If it's not an emphatic, exciting "Heck, yes!" then it's a no. Now not all of us are at the stage of our career when we can make those types of decisions. Many of us are still in the "I'll do anything I get asked to for the experience and the exposure" stage. That's okay. But I've used this as a test for whether I'm supposed to say yes or no. How excited am I about the opportunity?

MULTITASKING? DON'T DO IT.

Multitasking. *It's a trap.*

You have probably fallen into this trap. Trying to do two things at once. Or fourteen things. Research would say that multitasking is one of the worst things you can do for your productivity.

With the smart phone and all its functions, and the access that technology provides, it's become nearly impossible not to try and multitask. But you must fight it. With everything you have. Focus is the key to getting things done.

Even the term multitasking is actually a misnomer. You actually can't do more than one thing at a time. It's not physically possible in reality. What we are actually doing is switching tasks. So the term that is used in the research is "task switching."

The brain works the best when it can focus on a single task for an extended period of time. Your best friend when it comes to productivity: *the airplane button.* So swipe up, hit the little airplane, turn your phone off and watch your productivity soar. Like an airplane.

10 results of multitasking/task switching:

1. Lower productivity by up to 40%[1]
2. Slower completion of the task
3. More errors in the task
4. The brain operates less efficiently
5. The brain can become overloaded
6. More stress
7. Less overall energy
8. Lower your IQ
9. Less fulfillment from a job well done
10. Can even damage your brain![2]

Travis Bradberry shares some sobering wisdom in a *Forbes* article. He writes: "A study at the University of London found that participants who multitasked during cognitive tasks experienced IQ score declines that were similar to what they'd expect if they had smoked marijuana or stayed up all night … in the average range of an 8-year-old child. So the next time you're writing your boss an email during a meeting, remember that your cognitive capacity is being diminished to the point that you might as well let an 8-year-old write it for you."[3]

One Exception

The only acceptable multitasking that research has uncovered is doing a physical task that you have done very often and are very good at, then you can do that physical task while you are doing a mental task. So if you have learned to walk well, then you can walk and talk at the same time. But even that is sometimes difficult. Good luck, and don't multitask!

EMAIL HACKS

Email, indiscriminate web surfing, and social media perusal are the biggest time-wasters of our modern time. Here are some tips to help you corral the email monster:

1. Work on emails in chunks. Only check your email twice per day and for a limited time. You'll become much more efficient at email that way. If you need to, put up a message (see Michael Hyatt's blog post about email addiction for a sample email "workday" responder). Have a specific time (or times) you check your email.
2. Only touch emails once. Read them one time and act on them.
3. Read over emails before sending. Don't send criticism. Praises should be carved in stone; criticism written in sand. That means such conversations should be had over the phone or in person if possible.
4. Find out your employer's expectations for email. When should you be checking it? When should you be available? How often on the weekend?

5. Apply the five Ds:
    + Destroy it. Delete it from your to do list. Not important enough.
    + Delegate it. Really let them own it.
    + Delay it. This is not procrastination. Moving something can be strategic.
    + Diminish it. Apply selective perfectionism. Remember that principle about the extra 10 percent.
    + Dive in to that important task. Do it.

While these apply to email, they can also be applied to tasks and projects.

GET A PRACTICAL DAILY RHYTHM

If you want to grow, you must put it in your schedule. No one drifts into growth. Imagine your day as a greenhouse. What are you doing to promote growth?

Here is my ideal morning routine. I actually do this less than half the time, but that's better than none of the time. If you win the morning, you win the day. Get in a routine where you don't have to make a lot of decisions.

1. Make your bed. Start with a small win, with accomplishing a task.
2. Breakfast. Start healthy.
3. Meditation, reading the Bible, prayer, silence, journaling (one hour).
4. Exercise (half hour to one hour).
5. One hour of growth. Investment in yourself. This usually looks like reading or writing, reflecting, and thinking. (Turn off your cell phone or have it on airplane mode. Tough to do. I cheat on this all the time.)
6. Determine if there's anything that will take less than three minutes to complete. If there is, knock it out. Consider the words of

Mark Twain: "If it's your job to eat a frog, it's best to do it first thing in the morning. And if it's your job to eat two frogs, it's best to eat the biggest one first."

7. Then I attack the most important question to ask: What is the most *important* thing for me to do today? Not tomorrow, not next week. Not the urgent thing, not necessarily the pressing thing, but the most important thing. If you only accomplish one thing today, what should it be? That's the first frog.

8. Then after that, think about the highest-leverage task on your list. What's the one that will have the biggest impact and the one that only you can do?

If you don't have hours of time in the morning, what can you do to focus your day? Even if you want to spend twenty-five minutes, you could be quiet/meditate for five minutes, read something inspirational for ten minutes, and then read something related to your work for ten minutes. You will then win the morning and that will help you win the day.

THE DAFFODIL PRINCIPLE

In her book *The Daffodil Principle: One Woman, Two Hands, One Bulb at a Time*, Jaroldeen Asplund Edwards tells a story that happened about seventy-five miles outside of Los Angeles:

We turned onto a small gravel road and I saw … a sign that said, "Daffodil Garden." … Before me lay the most glorious sight. It looked as though someone had taken a great vat of gold and poured it down over the mountain peak and slopes. The flowers were planted in majestic, swirling patterns-great ribbons and swaths of deep orange, white, lemon yellow, salmon pink, saffron, and butter yellow … five acres of flowers. A sign hung … "Answers to the Questions I Know You Are Asking."

"50,000 bulbs," it read. The second answer was, "One at a time, by one woman. Two hands, two feet, and very little brain." The third answer was, "Began in 1958."

There it was, The Daffodil Principle. ... This woman whom I had never met, more than forty years before, had begun—one bulb at a time—to bring her vision of beauty and joy to an obscure mountain top. Still, just planting one bulb at a time, year after year, had changed the world. ... She had created something of magnificence, beauty, and inspiration.[4]

Some of you might be filled with regret after hearing this short story. Feeling like you should have started something grand a while ago. But it's never too late to start! Today is the first day of the rest of your life. Time is on your side. You have your whole life in front of you. It doesn't matter where you've come from. It doesn't matter your background. You can accomplish great things. You were meant to accomplish great things. Everyone has greatness within them. The challenge is drawing it out.

Some people hope to be lucky. Overnight sensations aren't built overnight. The "lucky" people did a lot of the small things for a long time before they were "lucky." The success might come quickly, but the blood, sweat, and tears do not. Michelangelo said, "If people knew how hard I worked to get my mastery, it wouldn't seem so wonderful at all."

Take my friend Bill for example. He is not a wealthy man, but he is very wise. Bill wrote me a letter every month starting when I got out of college—full of encouragement and wisdom, and a check for $50 to the nonprofit I was working for. Do you know that before he had to stop writing because he turned ninety and was unable to write anymore, he had given over $10,000! Not to mention hundreds of letters dripping of wisdom and insight. His faithfulness has been an incredible picture to me.

Then there's two of my best friends from college—let's call them Charles and Algood. For over twenty years, they've played in almost every one of my golf fundraisers for the nonprofit I work for. Together they've raised over $60,000! Working every year, a little bit at a time. Many lives have been changed because of the faithfulness of these men.

Utilize the daffodil principle. One action done repeatedly and faithfully can make a tremendous difference. Little things done over and over can become big things. You are the sum of your time. Get after it. Win the morning. Get the right habits and take some big swings. Then watch over the long haul as you accomplish great things.

THE BIG 3

- A little, over a long time, can be a lot.
- Ask what the most important thing is to do that day, and attack it.
- Win the morning, win the day.

17

#SMARTGOALS

It was a gorgeous October morning. The air was a brisk fifty-five degrees. The birds were chirping. The sun was out. And Miguel was running. He had been running for three miles, and the finish line was in sight. Hundreds of people were lined up, welcoming him to the end of the race. He and three of his coworkers were finishing their first 5K. The feelings of exhaustion, excitement, accomplishment, and pride quickly overwhelmed him. He set out to accomplish a goal nearly ten months prior, and today was its culmination.

At the end of 2012, I (Josh) sat down with the leadership team I had assembled at Chick-fil-A. During that year, we had become much better at setting goals for our restaurant and chasing after them. Throughout the process I realized that we didn't require our leaders to set goals personally; they were required professionally but nothing more. This was a huge miss because so many of them were not actively pursuing growth on their own. We spent several meetings learning about goal setting and how it impacts people's lives. At the end of the third meeting, they had a deadline: January 1, 2013.

Knowing how to set and pursue goals will change your life. This sounds like one of those miserably boring topics, like creating a budget, that you just want to avoid. Trust me, I understand.

In college, Pete (the coauthor of this book) required everyone working for him in the nonprofit he ran to submit semester goals. He was so strict on this requirement that no one was allowed to lead Young Life at their respective schools until they submitted typed goals to him. You're reading that correctly—we weren't allowed to be volunteers donating our time, energy, and money until we submitted personal goals to him.

At first, I was frustrated, as were my friends. It seemed ridiculous. Why on earth did I need to do something as silly as sending in goals? I was a college student with a million other things to worry about, and they impacted me a whole lot more than just writing some stuff on paper I would never look at. I could write out my goals or spend that time studying for my upcoming discrete mathematics test (bonus life wisdom—don't be a math major in college like I was). If I failed that test, no amount of goal setting would prevent me from taking a victory lap (a fifth year) at JMU.

Pete started the conversation around this requirement of goal setting by first telling us how we should build out this set of goals. Most everyone in the room had never done anything like this before, so setting up some guidelines would prove to be valuable. First, we started with topics. What did we care about? For each person, it was a little different. We started by thinking about the areas in life that we cared about the most, then narrowed down the number of topics to five to seven. Here are some of mine:

- School
- Physical health
- Spirituality
- Finances
- Relationships—family, friends
- Mental activities—hobbies, reading
- Fun—the best part

Now it's your turn. Once you've figured out the categories that are most important, determine what it is you want to accomplish over the upcoming length of time (month, semester, year, etc.). Then narrow down what it is you want to do and create a goal that is much more powerful by making it SMART.

SMART is a commonly used goal-building acronym that stands for:

- Specific. Is the goal specific? *I want to be a better person* is not specific. *I want to run a 5k* is a much more specific starting point.
- Measurable. At the end, can you say, "Yes, I accomplished this" or "No, I didn't"?
- Ambitious. Does this stretch you beyond what's easy?
- Realistic. Is it something that can be physically accomplished? It is great to have the goal to get to the moon by this summer. Probably not within the realm of possibility though.
- Time sensitive. This is crucial. Your goal must have an end date. No end date, no goal.

Let's take a goal and make it SMART. Often, I will hear a person say something like, "I want to get a job" or "I want to learn Spanish." Even looking at these two becomes challenging because there's no clue where to begin. Both are goals, but because the SMART filter hasn't been applied, it's nearly impossible to move forward with intentionality. Let's take the second example and apply the SMART filter.

"I want to learn Spanish." By when? How? The first thing to do is make the goal specific. "I want to learn Spanish *by* using Rosetta Stone." All right, now for making it measurable. You want to be able to say yes or no when you look back at this goal. "I want to learn Spanish *by* using Rosetta Stone *for* thirty minutes five times each week."

Is this ambitious in your current stage of life? If you grew up in Mexico, then this wouldn't be an ambitious goal. But if you're attempting to learn a second language, then it's absolutely ambitious. Is it a realistic goal? I would venture to say that if you live in the United States, this goal would be relevant to most places, and you have the capacity to learn this language.

Finally, make it time sensitive. "I want to learn Spanish *by* using Rosetta Stone *for* thirty minutes five times each week *until* June 30." It's critical to give yourself a deadline that you can look toward. Without a deadline, it doesn't really stir a passion to accomplish.

Now let's look back at where we started. "I want to learn Spanish" became "I want to learn Spanish by using Rosetta Stone for thirty minutes five times each week until June 30." Which one gives a clearer objective and plan? Which one ignites excitement and passion?

Learning how to set goals from a young age will propel you past your peers and give you a tangible way to continue to learn and better yourself. There are a ton of different objectives you have for your life that you will "just remember." No! Write them down and get after them. The power of writing down your goals is unparalleled. And then put those goals in a place where you'll see them. Last, share them with other people. Tell your closest friends what you're trying to achieve and ask for their help holding you accountable. Starting to make goals at a young age will be a life-altering event as you progress into your adult years.

THE BIG 3

- Write down five SMART goals.
- Tell other people what your goals are and give them a copy of them.
- Make your goals stir a passion inside of you.

PART 7

FOUNDATIONS

18

#THETOPBUTTON

What are you trying to get out of life? What about your goals this year? Did you have a New Year's resolution? How are you doing with it? Ever wonder what other people want to change or accomplish?

You might be interested to know the most searched New Year's resolutions on Google for 2017 (thanks to the data company iQuanti):

- "Get Healthy"—over 62 million searches
- "Get Organized"—over 33 million searches
- "Live Life to the Fullest"—nearly 19 million searches
- "Learn New Hobbies"—over 17 million searches
- "Spend Less/Save More"—nearly 16 million searches
- "Travel"—nearly 6 million searches
- "Read More"—over 4 million searches[1]

We want to thank you for reading this book. It was written with a deep desire to see you succeed and make it in this next season of your life. Our intention is to help you accomplish number three—to live life to the fullest. We hope you've been inspired to be who you were meant to be. We hope you have more clarity about your purpose and passions. And we hope you're motivated to "do good" and make an impact wherever you land. Remember to:

- Be the friend you wish you had.
- Be the employee you wish you had.
- Be the boss you wish you had.
- Be the coworker you wish you had.
- Be the family member you wish you had.

- Be the leader you wish you had.
- Be the support you wish you had.

You're seeking a life well lived. You're seeking a life of meaning and impact and significance. This comes from influencing people. Because at the end of the game, all the toys go back in the box. Have you ever seen the bumper sticker that says *He who dies with the most toys wins*? I wish it had next to it a coffin with a bunch of toys on it. An iPhone. A Monopoly game. And an Xbox sitting on top of the casket. You can't enjoy anything when you're dead. You don't get to take it with you.

Remember the cigar guy from the very first chapter, Jack? He would ask me, "Have you ever seen a hearse pulling a U-Haul?" all the time. He would also ask, "How does God feel about you right now?" To end this book, we want to talk about the *why*. The *why* you would do good. The *why* of this book. The *why* of life. It's related to what we think about God. It's related to what you think about God. Because what you think about God is the most important thing about you. It will determine everything else. It's like the top button of a shirt.

What you believe is the foundation for how you engage with others, where you spend your time, and how you leverage your finances. Every area in life that we have touched on throughout this book builds out from what we believe matters most.

Everything Josh and I have shared has a common thread—the person of Jesus is central in our lives. Many would say he is the most influential man who ever lived. He never commanded an army or led a country, but he did lead a revolution. His name was Jesus. And before you throw this book down in frustration, give me a chance to explain why I think he is worthy of your intense investigation. Let me share with you four brief facts that should compel you to know more:

Fact #1: *Jesus' biography is the best-selling book ever written.* This book is the Bible. There are more copies of the Bible sold every year than the number one best seller, and the numbers aren't even close. Could there be something in the Bible worth your time? Maybe something about the recipe for success in life? Who is the world's most prolific writer in the last twenty years? J. K. Rowling, the Harry Potter juggernaut. She has seven of the top ten most-sold books over the last twenty years. How many books did she sell? Over 500 million. That's a lot. But the Bible has sold more copies in that same time period. Something in it seems to be compelling to vast numbers of humans. Could Jesus be worth a closer look?

Fact #2: *Most of the world dates time after Jesus.* If you're an important person, when you die, people might name a building or street after you. Or even a whole city. If you're of utmost importance to a nation, you might get your picture on the currency. But when you die and people decide to start time, then you're the most important person who has ever lived. When my friend Sloop dies, if he is the most important person to ever have lived, they will start time again. Instead of B.C. (before Christ), it will be B.S. (before Sloop). We know this won't happen, even though he is a great guy. No one has lived a life like Jesus. Could Jesus be worth a closer look?

Fact #3: *Jesus' name has uncanny power.* If you go in any locker room or attend a sporting event, you will hear his name a lot. Maybe you said his name recently in a moment of stress or duress. Or when you stubbed your toe or hit your finger with a hammer or hurt yourself or heard something outrageous. You might say, "Jesus Christ!" Why do you do this? Why do I do this? This man lived in poverty on the other side of the world (from the United States) over two thousand years ago. And yet we say his name in moments of increased agitation or passion. Why do we do this? Doesn't this seem odd? Could Jesus be worth a closer look?

Fact #4: *More goodwill and charity has been done in his name than any other.* And the comparison is not even close. More hospitals, food pantries, shelters, orphanages, nonprofits, etc. have been started in Jesus' name than any other. This is very convincing for me. This is persuasive. Could Jesus be worth a closer look?

THE TOP BUTTON OF YOUR LIFE

The big question is why? Why does Jesus have these stats? Have you ever been buttoning a shirt or a blouse and gotten to the bottom to find you have an extra button? You look in the mirror and your collar is sitting all weird, and you realize that you started with the wrong button. If the first one is off, every other one will be off. It's the same way with what you think about Jesus. If you get that one wrong, every other part of your life will be off. You won't become who you were meant to be. He is the top button.

Who do you say that he is? Your answer to that question will be the top button of your life. It will determine everything else. It will determine how you think about reality. It will determine how you treat other people. It will determine how you spend your money and your time.

I want you to have an accurate picture of who this man was and is. He came in love. He came to save the world and not condemn it. He came to offer grace and truth and love for every human being on the planet.

As I was working on this book, an insane act of terror happened when someone drove their car into a crowd in Charlottesville, Virginia. The crowd had gathered as a response to a neo-Nazi white supremacist nationalist demonstration. I was especially struck by this tragic, unspeakable, horrendous, cowardly act because I went to college in Charlottesville at the University of Virginia. My first reaction was that I wanted to drive a car into whoever did this. And pay them back. An eye for an eye. But our first reactions are often not the correct reactions.

My second response was anger and confusion. Why would they do this? How could they do this? One of the foundational beliefs of these supremacists is that their race is better than all the other races in the world. They don't believe in the value of every human life. This violates something that most of us know to be true—that every person, regardless of their race, religion, physical or mental capabilities, background, beliefs, etc. is of infinite worth. Everyone has dignity. Did you know that this is an explicit belief of Jesus? Did you also know that no other world religion or philosophy has sufficient grounds or basis to believe this? If you believe that life is by chance or humans developed by mistake, then life is meaningless. If you believe that when people die they cease to exist, then life is meaningless (in the grand scheme). Let's come at it from a different angle.

From Something or Nothing?

Something exists now.
Something cannot come from nothing.
Therefore, something must have always existed.

Science would say something never comes from nothing. Things may be reclassified, reorganized, and even transformed, but there cannot be a case of some being coming into existence from nothing.

So everyone needs to answer the question, "What is the something that has always existed?"

Furthermore, if you believe the human race happened by chance and that life ceases to exist when we die, that means we came from nothing, and we're going to nothing, and in between we were by chance. Or a mistake of molecules. So, if we come from nothing and we're going to nothing, guess what's in between? Nothing. I'm sorry, but your life has no meaning, purpose, or significance.

But there is another school of thought. If we were created with meaning, purpose, and significance, and after we die there is meaning and purpose and significance, guess what we have in the middle during our life here? Yes, you're right! Meaning, purpose, and significance. And you know in your heart that this is the case.

These are some of the things that make us human. This is an explicit Christian belief. The supremacists got it wrong. Everyone has tremendous value. No other world religion or way of thought has the basis for the dignity of the human race. Each one of us has been created with a divine spark. In the image of God. This is Jesus' view of humanity. Could he be worth a closer look?

This World Isn't as It Should Be

One last thought-provoking truth. Our world is messed up. That's one thing we can all agree on. Extreme acts of terror have occurred recently in Paris, Barcelona, London, and several cities in the United States. And extreme violence within the United States threatens to tear the fabric of our country apart. This isn't the way it was meant to be. The world is not the way it was supposed to be.

If you believe that there's a way it was meant to be, where did you get that idea? How do you know what *right* is? Or what is *good*? This argument depends on evil and suffering being objectively bad, but according to John Stonestreet and G. Shane Morris, "if we're merely subatomic particles, then no arrangement of those particles can be morally better or worse than any other … we know better. The world is broken. It's not functioning according to God's original design … the blame is on humanity's rebellion against the Creator."[2]

We believe this comes from God and is written on our heart. And each one of us has rebelled in some way against what is good and right. That's why our world has the problems it does. The problem with the world is me.

So if you don't believe this, have you come up with a better answer to why the world is messed up? Don't you think we would have worked out a solution? With all the incredibly intelligent men and women who have lived before us, why does it feel like sometimes we're going backward? The answer doesn't lie in politics, education, trying harder, being better, or any of those tired options. It's something else completely—something that most of the people of the world have not heard about in its fullness or are not willing to embrace. The answer is a person. The most important person who ever lived. Could Jesus be worth a closer look?

UNLOCKED AND UNLEASHED

The recipe for success in this life is following Jesus. Not just a successful life but an incredible, exciting, adventuresome, full life. Remember that third New Year's resolution at the beginning of the chapter? It's the way life was meant to be lived. You'll never be who you were meant to be until you start following Jesus. He unlocks and unleashes your heart and soul in a way that cannot be overstated. He's not just a good teacher; he's someone you should trust with your very life.

And just as what you think about God is so important, what he thinks about you might be even more important. The more I heard about what God thought of me, the less I cared about what people thought of me. And this is the wild part: God knows every little detail about you. He knows everything you've ever done or thought. Even that one thing that you think no one knows, he knows all about it. And he loves you. In fact, he can't love you any more, and he won't love you any less. It is a radical, relentless, pursuing, and extravagant love. The way to live life to the fullest is through following not just the teachings of Jesus but the actual person of Jesus himself.

We still like you no matter what you decide about Jesus. No matter what faith you are, if any. We still want you to succeed. But we also want you to experience life the way it was meant to be lived. To meet the One who knows you deeper than any other person can or will, and who loves you. He is what you've been looking for. But don't take our word for it, try it out. Investigate. Ask questions. Be curious. Doubt. Risk. Be bold. Take a chance. Live life to the fullest. We wish you the best. We want you to step into who you were meant to be and make a huge difference in our world. You were made for this.

#YOUKNOWYOUAREANADULTWHEN

This is a sampling from six pages of life wisdom that Pete gave to me (Josh) in a grocery store nearly a decade ago; these became the inspiration for this entire project. Below are a smattering of random tips, tricks, and life advice that Pete wanted us young leaders to know before we went into the "real world."

Marriage

- Ask *if* you should get married, not *who* you should marry.
- Become the person the person you are looking for is looking for.
- Don't be in a rush to find someone to marry.
- Don't marry until you're established as an individual.
- Your mate complements but never completes you.
- Don't look for fulfillment in life from someone else; that isn't their job.
- Soul mates are created, not found.
- Marriage is a discipline, a commitment; it's much more than a feeling.

Mental

- Do hard things.
- Start the habit of reading. Leaders are learners and leaders are readers. You can spend time with anyone in the world by reading their books.
- Read stuff you want to read fast while standing up.

- Meditate and think more. Reflect more. Howard Hendricks said of every hour reading, forty minutes should be reading and twenty minutes should be reflecting.
- You'll be like the five people you spend the most time with.
- When you have a person you can't take no from or say no to, you have, in effect, handed over the control of your life to them.
- Have a mind-set dedicated to growing yourself.
- Hang around really smart people.
- Dream big. Take big swings at things.
- Do one extraordinary thing every day.
- Don't pull all-nighters; it never works.

Leadership

- Delegation is a key to being a leader. It is an art.
- Write compliments down, share criticism verbally.
- Never insult someone by giving them an easy job.
- Discipleship: People will think, feel, talk, act your example.
- "Instruction is what we say. Influence is what we do. Image is what we are."[1]
- Availability, ability, and attitude: look for these in employees.
- Your growth rate in revenue can't outpace your growth rate in people.
- The best people don't need to be managed. Led, yes, but not managed.
- Lead with questions, not answers.
- Engage in dialogue and debate, not coercion.
- If you don't change, you become extinct.
- What you're afraid of is never as bad as what you imagine.
- Feelings are great friends but terrible masters.
- People don't care how much you know until they know how much you care.
- Leaders don't create followers, they create more leaders.

- People don't leave organizations, they leave leaders.
- When you put out someone's candle, it doesn't make yours any brighter.
- "Failure is not an option. … It is a privilege reserved exclusively for those who try."[2]
- True failure only happens when you quit.
- You are doing something today because of a decision you made yesterday.
- If you truly tried your best, it would be obvious to us—but saying you did makes us think you failed and could have tried harder.
- Failure is always a learning experience. Just don't fail because of lack of preparation.
- Life isn't just about showing up, and whiners don't win.
- Courage is not letting your reality determine your reaction.
- Losers react, leaders anticipate.
- Winners take responsibility, losers blame others.
- To be a great leader, you have to be great at home with your family first.
- True success is when those closest to you and most important to you love you and respect you the most.
- Have a personal growth plan. If you fail to plan, you plan to fail. If you aim at nothing you'll hit it every time.
- Live a multicultural life. Extend yourself in at least one friendship to a person who is different from you in ethnicity, background, sexual preference, etc.

Professionalism

- Get to know the secretaries, assistants, and administrators. They are the gatekeepers and incredibly important, valuable people.
- Shake hands firmly, every time.
- When in doubt, shave and dress up. You don't regret overdressing as much as underdressing.

- Dress how you want to get treated.
- Act how you want to be treated.
- Dress right. You don't get a second chance to make a first impression.
- If you call someone and don't leave a message, you're communicating you don't want a call back.
- Have a professional message on your voicemail.
- Never go into a meeting blind. Do some recon to find out what the meeting is about or what the person wants to meet about.
- Never use family members as references.
- Use a professional email account.
- Dress professionally at every stage while pursuing a job (dropping off an application/ interviews).
- Your career is a marathon, not a sprint.
- Have your voicemail set up.
- Hard work and a positive attitude will propel you in your career.
- Your first job is not your final job.
- In every job, always strive to do more than what you are paid for.

Weddings

- You're supposed to send a gift when you're invited, not just when you go.
- You have a year to send/give the present for a wedding.
- RSVP early and every time.
- Always arrive at weddings (and funerals) at least forty-five minutes early.

Attire

- Your tie should come to your belt buckle.
- Buy stuff you really want to wear.
- Get two or three great outfits, especially one suit.

Email/Voicemail

- At the end of every email, ask, *Is there anyone else who should see this?*
- Read over emails before sending them out.
- Get in the habit of adding the recipient last. The email can't get sent mistakenly with no recipient.
- Back up your computer every month—get an external hard drive or iCloud subscription.
- Get an email address that will last beyond college. Make the transition now.
- Save or delete your emails. Don't crowd your inbox. If it calls for action, keep it.
- Always look at attachments before sending.
- Beware of the *Reply all* button.
- Find out your employer's expectation for email. When should you be checking it? Over the weekend?
- Have a specific time you check email (for example, one hour per day).
- Keep emails short.
- Try to communicate your message in the subject line.

Time Management

- First things first.
- You must prioritize. Put the big rocks in first.
- If you're not sure if a store is open, call before you go.
- Plan out your days and weeks. Ten minutes of planning saves an hour of time.
- If a commitment is more than a week old, call that morning to reconfirm.
- Be early, everywhere.
- If you want to remember something, put your keys with it.
- Take a book everywhere you go, just in case you get somewhere and you have time to kill.

- Ask yourself, *Am I the right person to be doing this?*
- Start big tasks with an easy step one (for example, even the word *start* is better).
- Construct a filing system that works for you. Keep important documents. (Use Evernote for digital filing.) Keep your tax returns for seven years.
- Treat yourself. Work hard for a half hour, then break for five minutes.
- If something's not pressing and you're unsure, wait.
- If something takes less than three minutes, do it immediately (especially emails).
- You need a place to write everything down, even easy stuff.
- Keep your planner next to you at all times, especially during quiet times, study times, and prayer.
- Get phone messages out of voicemail ASAP and into a to-do list.
- Call people back within twenty-four hours. If you can't call back within forty-eight hours, put a message on your phone (and your email) that you'll be unable to get messages for a while. Use the automatic email response feature.
- Be busy but not in a rush. Eliminate hurry from your life.
- There will always be more to do.
- Schedule everything; don't just create a to-do list.
- You can always make time for what you care about the most.
- Every yes to something is a no to something else.
- Don't ask how can I do this, but rather, how can this get done?
- Don't do anything that isn't the best use of your time.
- "If you think you can or if you think you can't, you're right" (Henry Ford).

Tips/Tricks

- Write down your friends' kids' names; they're hard to remember.
- When you stay at people's houses or borrow things, leave them better then when you found them.

- When you go to dinner at someone's house, bring something (flowers, wine, dessert).
- "If I went back to college again, I'd concentrate on two areas: learning to write and to speak before an audience. Nothing in life is more important than the ability to communicate effectively."[3]
- Smile. Say hi first. Relax first.
- Always have a pen and paper with you.
- Start getting up early. How many influential people do you know who slept in and stayed up really late?
- Remember people's names. Repeat their name while talking; it helps.
- Get around the people you want to be like and ask them lots of questions.
- You will not regret making sacrifices to be at the special happenings in people's lives.
- Learn by asking questions.
- Set written goals. The top 3 percent of people in any field have written out their goals.
- *Imagine* is a good word to use.
- Guys, always put the toilet lid down. Some people don't care, but to others it's a big deal.
- Revive the lost art of letter-writing.
- Call people and friends with no agenda and just to see how they are doing.
- Start a rainy-day file full of encouraging notes or cards that you have received.
- Start a page with *Someday Maybe* as the title—these are dreams that you want to accomplish.
- Knock on any closed door. You never know what's behind it.
- Be genuinely interested in other people.
- You can't always do great things, but you can do small things with great love.

- You're learning not just for you but for everyone you will ever meet.
- Clean your dryer lint screen every time you use the dryer, and leave your washer open as soon as it's done.
- Always get a home inspection.
- Men, open the door for women.
- Everyone, hold the door for the person behind you.
- Do one extraordinary thing every day. It adds up.

Car

- Oil change at every three thousand miles (unless you have synthetic oil).
- Tire rotation/balance every six thousand miles. Many places will do free tire rotations for life.
- Preventative maintenance is the best kind. Do stuff right the first time.
- Know how to change a tire.
- Know how to change your oil.
- Any expense over $1000, get a second opinion.
- Find a mechanic you trust.
- Always fill up your car at a quarter of a tank. Never wait until empty.
- Have a pair of jumper cables in your car. You never know what will happen, and it's fun to help strangers out.
- Don't leave anything on the seats of your car.

Grocery Store

- Pay attention to the price per unit. It's the only thing that matters. That's how you compare prices between products.
- Grocery list—always have it with you. (Use your phone.)
- Never grocery shop when you're hungry.
- Check your top four or five favorites every time. If they're on sale, stock up.

- Lunch meats and cheeses—ask the deli workers which one is better (they will usually even let you sample them).
- Make a big meal for the whole week. A little in the fridge, a little in the freezer in containers.
- Clip coupons and keep them all together in an envelope for grocery shopping.
- Consider what you're paying yourself per hour as you look for deals. Make sure it's worth it.
- Beware of buying in bulk. It can be a huge winner but has its pitfalls.

Financial

- There's more written on money in the Bible than on heaven and hell combined.
- We are temporary stewards. We are managers of God's property. No ownership.
- Recommended investment order:
  + Matching 401K (or any match from employer).
  + Roth IRA.
  + Emergency fund to cover two to three months of expenses.
  + Car fund. Even if it's a small amount. Save every month.
- The difference between rich and poor is two cents. The rich make $1.00 and spend $0.99. The poor make $1.00 and spend $1.01.
- Pay off credit cards immediately. Give everything you have to get out of this debt. A mortgage and student loans should be the only debt you have.
- Start investing right away. Right now. Even if it's $25 per month. Do it.
- *Buy low, sell high* is counterintuitive, but it's the right thing with stocks.
- Write financial goals down.
- Give generously. You can't out-give God (See Malachi 3:9–10).

- Set up investments for automatic deduction. It's easier when you don't have to think about it and it automatically comes out.
- Tip generously. God has all the money in the world.
- Spend some time calling around when making an expensive purchase. If you save $20 and it took you twenty minutes, you just paid yourself $60 an hour.
- Shop for presents year-round. If you find something that's an incredible deal, buy it and keep it in a box.
- A budget is a moral document.
- Don't look through Amazon or catalogs when you don't need anything.
- Don't browse in stores where you don't need stuff.
- Money is a good servant but a bad master.
- It's not what you make but what you keep.
- Success leaves clues. Model those you want to be like.
- Serve people. Give to people who can't pay you back.
- Learn how to write a check.

HOW TO CRUSH COLLEGE

In high school, everything was planned out for you—when you started the school day, when you ate, when you practiced, etc. In college: You. Are. Free. This can be good or this can be bad. It's up to you. Make it good. Make it the best four to six-plus years of your life so far. Take some time to be carefree and careless, but also take time to develop yourself. Explore your interests, passions, gifts, and talents, and learn how you're wired.

We polled a group of people who have over two hundred years of combined experience working with college students and asked their top five pieces of advice for an incoming freshman. Here are their top answers, combined with some of our thoughts.

STUDYING, CLASS, AND ACADEMIC ADVICE

- Schedule classes in blocks, with little breaks in between. Only break for meals. Once you get your momentum going, you want to keep it going.
- Don't study in your room. Find your study place. This should be where no one can find you and where you can focus and rid yourself of distractions and disruptions. What will take you one hour in the library will take you two to three hours in your dorm room or a social library.
- Go to office hours. This shows initiative, interest, and work ethic. Often professors will give hints or really focus your study time. Ask what will be on the exam. And if your grade is ever on the edge, the fact that you came to office hours may help you.

- Schedule your free time. Seize your time. Learn to put in your schedule the things you need to do, instead of just making a to-do list. Put things in your schedule and allot a certain amount of time for them. Schedule the times and places for study; for example, *From four to five p.m., I will work on my chemistry project.* Be specific. This can help alleviate that constant, low-level anxiety about something you think you should be doing.
- Don't study in groups. A couple of days before an exam, you can get together with a group for a limited time if you want to *review* and go over the material. Tell the group that you will not be studying together, but reviewing together.
- Study in hour-long chunks. Study for about fifty minutes and then take a ten-minute break. Reset your learning curve. This is difficult to do. But get in the habit. Set a timer for fifty minutes and then one for ten minutes.
- Get around some high-achievers. This will stretch you, challenge you, and inspire you. Ask them their habits, their techniques, how they think about schoolwork, what inspires them, etc.
- Learn how to set deadlines for yourself. Aren't you already a pro at meeting deadlines? When a paper or a project is due, you always rally at the last minute. Now the key will be to divide up the work and set deadlines for yourself to finish portions of this project/paper before the night before.

THOUGHTS FROM THE BOOK *HOW TO WIN AT COLLEGE*, BY CAL NEWPORT

- Anyone can become a standout student if they learn what is required and are willing to put in the work.
- Master the skill of skimming thoroughly. At first, err on the side of reading as much as possible, but then fine-tune the art of pulling out the most important and relevant information.

- Most of the test material will come from class.
- Drop classes every semester. Get out of bad classes. Get into good ones.
- Start on long-term projects the day they are assigned. Thirty minutes. Write out a schedule, an outline, just do something.
- Find one thing that you can be the best at.
- Pick one project or one test per semester per class, and *smash* it. Blow the curve. Stand out.[1]

THE BIG PICTURE

- Start strong. The first three weeks usually set the standard for the foreseeable future. Do your best to get into a regular pattern of classes, study, recreation, and rest. Don't get behind in classes. Keep up, especially early on.
- Get a good GPA the first semester. It's really difficult to recover from a poor GPA in the first semester or first year. Do your best to get good grades at the beginning. And then the good news is each semester counts a little less toward your total GPA. The first semester GPA is 100 percent of your total GPA at that time. Second semester then is only 50 percent of your total GPA at that time and so on.
- The Four-Year Test: When you graduate, as the measure for how you want your first month to look, think about what you want people to say about you four years later.
- The Morning Test: How you feel about the night before is largely felt the next day. If you regret or don't feel good about things, don't do them again.
- Begin the practice of saying no. Consider saying no to something every day. Especially in college, there is *always* something to do: someone wants to hang out, watch a movie, go to the quad. If you can learn to say no to things when you need to, it will make you more effective and able to develop deeper relationships. This will help you learn to under-promise and

over-deliver. If you learn the art of saying no early, you'll end up hurting fewer people than if you try to say yes to everything.

- Before you get to college, have a conversation with someone you respect about what your hopes and dreams are. Make sure you remind yourself of your identity often. This helps you decide who you want to be instead of having others or circumstances dictate who you are.

- Be aware/careful about what you put on social media. Assume future employers will be able to see everything.

- Choose friends by your priorities, not your priorities by your new friends. In the rush to make friends, freshmen often bond with the first people they meet and without thought begin to engage in whatever activities their new friends do. Decide what is important to you (grades, faith, etc.) and find some friends who share those priorities.

- Emotionally go to college. Many freshmen don't have a good experience because they're not there emotionally. You can stay in touch with your friends from high school, but this is a different chapter of life. Make sure to be fully present and invested in where you are.

- Become part of a group. Studies and surveys indicate the happiest and most successful students are part of a campus group that shares their goals and priorities. If you are a person of faith, find and connect with a group on your campus immediately.

- Make the most of your summers. They are gifts. Of course you should rest and relax and do something carefree like road trip to Philly, eat a cheesesteak, then turn around and road trip back home. But you have three months to develop and explore and adventure. If you need to get a job, try to get one that is interesting. Not just your pizza-delivery or lifeguarding job from high school. Shadow someone for a week in an industry that interests you. But most of all, have a plan. Plan your summer. Those who fail to plan, plan to fail. And depending on your financial situation, this is the time to really hunker down and make as much money as you can.

- How many people wake up in the morning and say to themselves, *I think I'll ruin my life today*? No one does this, but lots of people end up in places and in situations they could never imagine—having not just made one terrible decision but also a bunch of small bad decisions. These compromises or lapses in judgment may land you in dangerous and damaging territory. Be vigilant and make the right small decisions to help you avoid the big bad decisions.

First Week

- In the first weeks of school, go to as many activities, clubs, and ministries as possible and see what interests you. This is a great time to try a bunch of different things. Don't limit yourself; see what interests you.
- Join a small group (regardless of where you are with your faith). Having a group to walk through life with is so helpful.
- Look for friends who want to talk about and experience real life and friendship. In high school, your friendships are based on what you do together (sports, clubs, etc.). In real life, your deepest friendships are based on common values. What do you really care about? What breaks your heart? What do you want to be about? Look for friends you want to keep forever. You don't have to be friends with people in your hall. You also don't need to be friends with everyone you meet. It's okay to be selective. Lasting relationships don't grow on trees. Even for the most independent person, the ones you choose as your main friends will inevitably shape who you become, so choose wisely.
- Wear shower shoes!

First Month

- Exercise. Find an activity, sport, or something active to engage in three to four times a week. You will not only be healthier, but it will help you focus on your school work, you will meet new people, and you will actually have *more* energy.
- Play intramurals. Never again in your life will you have so many opportunities to play so many different sports, team sports, with no practice, just games. "We talkin' bout practice!"
- Go on the Young Life College fall weekend if you have Young Life at your university. It will be the time of your life, and you will meet so many great new people.
- Connect with the people your mentors (parents, teachers, coaches, Young Life leaders, etc.) want you to meet.
- Go to student organization night.
- Don't go home. Even if you're lonely or homesick or really missing your family, stick it out. These first weeks are priceless in making new connections and relationships.

First Semester

- Decide not to date during the first semester. Find friends first, because if you spend all your time with one person and it doesn't work out, you may be left with no one. If you're already dating someone, give each other space. Don't hang out every day or go visit them every weekend. College is when you make deep friendships, and it's sad when someone hangs out with their significant other too much and never ends up making those lifelong friends. (And you usually don't end up with that person anyway!)
- You can do so much free stuff in college. Lots of schools let you sign out canoes, kayaks, mountain bikes, tents, etc., or they do crazy things like bring professional masseuses to campus or host concerts or whatever. You can do so many free things. Go do all the free things (that are legal).

- Don't pick your major because it makes money. Pick one that you love. Find your passion and where that meets a need in the world and choose to do that. Money really isn't everything.
- Find a place to serve. This will ground you in a sometimes turbulent and overwhelming time and give you purpose.
- Take a road trip. Every semester.
- At first, try everything. Explore lots of organizations, groups, meetings, etc. But long-term give your all to a few. Have a goal to go deep in a few places.

First Year

- Go to sporting events no matter how big/small or successful your school is at the time. It's fun.
- Don't use credit cards. Use your debit card.
- Take risks. Try things that are new for you and see what you like.
- Mountains of student loans allow you to have no responsibility and lots of fun for four years, but they will crush you for the next twenty. Try to take as little loan money as possible.

EXHORTATION TO COLLEGE FRESHMEN
FROM DR. TIMOTHY DALRYMPLE, HARVARD PHD

- Seek wisdom, not merely intelligence.
- Seek mentors, not merely teachers.
- Seek the truth, not merely prevailing opinion.
- Seek answers, not merely questions.
- Seek betterment, not merely achievement.
- Seek fellowship, not merely friends.[2]

A LETTER FROM PETE

Dear College Incoming Freshman,
You are about to embark on one of the craziest adventures of your life. College will be a blast, and it will change things. You will change and transform.

You'll probably change your major once, or three times like me. You might fall in love. Or out of it. The question is who will you be after these four-plus years? What will happen to your inner person? What about your character? Here are my top ten things you need to know. In no particular order:

1. *You matter. Your life matters. What you do for the next four years matters. Your decisions have consequences. You're shaping who you will be for the rest of your life.*

2. *You were meant to change the world. You aren't totally sure about this, but let me confirm what you've already been feeling. You were meant to make a difference. You were meant to have an impact.*

3. *Use these next four to seven years to find out who you are.*

   + *Invest some time in your spiritual growth. Does God exist? If so, what is God like? "Who is God?" might be the most important question you answer in life.*

   + *Find your "Yoda" or even a couple of mentors who are a little older and a couple of steps ahead of you. Learn everything you can from them.*

   + *Find out what matters to you and what you are excited about. Try all kinds of stuff—not drugs or anything weird, but different interests, organizations, clubs, etc.*

   + *You have certain innate talents that make you feel alive. Explore and develop these. Find out your strengths, weaknesses, passions, blind spots, and liabilities.*

4. *Learn how to study.*

   + *Only cram on stuff you don't want to retain. Then ask yourself,* Why am I taking this class in the first place?

   + *Go to class. Sit near the front (this will help you stay awake and pay attention). If it's terrible, study during class or do other work.*

   + *Talk to professors and meet with them. Go to office hours and ask how to study and how to do well in their class. Know your class policies/how grades are determined inside and out.*

    ✦ *Go to review sessions. Sometimes little "secrets" are given away.*

5. *Learn time management. You only get one shot at life, only one time through. Don't you want to get the most out of life? Choose people over program and sometimes over more immediate responsibilities. Hey, you're in college!*

6. *Figure out a way to serve. How can you give back? It really is in giving that we receive. That's not just a cheesy line, it's a profound truth.*

7. *Sex is really, really good. Fantastic, actually. But it is not to be trifled with. It's meant for two people who are committed to each other for life. There is no such thing as casual sex, and it is not just physical.*

8. *Meet everyone you can early on. Knock awkwardly on the doors of your hallmates. Plan hangouts. Take advantage of living in such close proximity to great people. And don't be afraid to make friends outside your dorm. Most of you will not live in a situation like this again. Everyone is waiting for someone to take the initiative.*

9. *Don't get a credit card. Don't buy anything you can't pay cash for. Use your debit card for all purchases.*

    ✦ *Start saving and investing.*
    ✦ *But also don't let money hold you back from something you want to do. Find a way to do it.*

10. *Be aware of your physical, emotional, and spiritual health. Exercise. Do intramural sports. Go easy on the all-you-can-eat part of dining. Eating three meals at all-you-can-eat is a recipe for disaster. Also, maybe don't have dessert with every meal.*

11. *Okay, I lied. I have eleven. Write down what you want to accomplish. It can be dumb stuff but also some serious hopes and dreams. Written goals are huge. There is power in written goals. Who do you want to become? What do you want to do? Get some clarity on what you want to make of these next four-plus years. Go for it! Dream big! Take risks! And have a blast. You were made for such a time as this. Many blessings to you on your journey.*

                             —*Pete Hardesty, former college student*

LIFE AFTER COLLEGE:
HOW TO ENTER THE REAL WORLD—MONTH 1

HIGH SCHOOL: "Don't tell me what to do."
COLLEGE: "I don't know what to do."
AFTER COLLEGE: "Please tell me what to do."

Basically, this book is geared toward you. But we thought we would put in a little bonus including some of the first things to do when you move into a new place and start your job in the "real world." You have way less discretionary time than you did in college (forty to fifty-plus hours a week is more than you spent in class and studying), so you must really learn to seize your time and plan well. As Paul Angone said, "You realize that success in your 20s and 30s is more about setting the table than enjoying the feast."[1]

TOP 10 THINGS YOU NEED TO DO THE FIRST MONTH

1. Get a handle on your money. Take a weekend to get a handle on your finances. Put everything in one place: all your accounts, balances, debts, loans, payments, etc. Get on a monthly budget ASAP. Sometime in the week before the next month starts, you should have a meeting with yourself (actually schedule it on your calendar so it happens). You'll plan out all your expenses for the following month. Start contributing to your employer account that matches; every month you wait is lost money that you cannot get back.

2. If you are person of faith, get connected. Go to your place of worship and get into a Bible study ASAP. Ask around and get as much info as you can. Push yourself even if you have to go alone. Explore a place to serve—maybe it's with a food kitchen, or through a church or nonprofit. Look for a place to give your life away, even if it's just a couple of hours a month. It will be a great way to meet some people in your new town, and it will help you to start a good pattern right away.

3. Work on discovering your passions. What are you excited about? What interests you? What are you good at? What are your gifts? Where is there a need in the world? Explore these and they could be sign posts to your next job or season of life. Find what you are passionate about and try something with it. It's okay if at first you find yourself just "working for the weekend." But look for something deeper. It could be your career or just a hobby, or a hobby that turns into a career down the road.

4. Set up a trip or reunion with your best friends and a trip to visit your family. Plan it now. Make family a priority; they are your family forever. Start some traditions. This sounds lame, but make a list of the people you want to make sure you stay in regular contact with. Maybe keep it in your car and instead of always listening to the radio, from time to time call your way down that list.

5. Work really hard at your job. Persevere. Have grit. This will help you accomplish what you want to achieve down the road. You have gone from top dog to underdog in about five seconds. Now go the extra mile. Do everything with excellence at work. Under-promise and over-deliver. Be spectacular. Hit a home run. Sometimes you can have an unrealistic perspective about your career and how fast it should grow. Make people take notice of you because of how responsive you are—email, phone calls, meetings, etc. Be humble. You don't know it all, but guess what? People at work who are older than you need you, your fresh perspective, and your skills with new technology.

6. Look for a constellation of mentors. Be hungry. Be willing to learn. Don't be entitled in the least. No one owes you anything. Not your job, or city, or friends, no one. Find a mentor—maybe someone you respect at your workplace, in your neighborhood, at church—and ask to learn from them. Don't ask to meet with them every week for three years. Start off with buying them lunch. And come ready with questions. Be a lifelong learner. Be a sponge, and soak up as much as you can. The world is a vast and fascinating tapestry. Let it blow you away. No one knows everything, so there is always something more to learn.

7. Accept that it's okay that it doesn't feel okay. It's weird. You might feel alone. Even in a big city. Life looks a lot different right after college—friendships especially. Community is built into the fabric of college whether you want it or not. Then the month after you graduate, you could be living alone or with roommates you barely know. It might take a while before you have relationships that are as deep as your college friends. My first year out of college I rented more movies from Blockbuster than most people do their whole life. I'm serious. I was a gold card member. That means you have to rent one hundred movies in a calendar year. But the good news is that it doesn't last forever. Consider seeking counseling, even if you aren't really depressed or feel like you need it. You really could learn some incredible things about yourself. The more self-aware you are, the better the friend, employee, husband/wife, mom/dad, sibling, etc. you will be.

8. Initiate. Be friendly to people. Reach out. Making friends is hard, but it is worth it. If you want friends, be a friend. Organize happy hours. Have a dinner party. It might take a couple of tiny gatherings or even things that no one comes to before you get a crew to do life with. That's okay. Decide what type of community you want to surround yourself with, and if it's not available to join, help create it.

9. Take risks! Dream big! Be willing to take risks, especially in your first couple of years out of college. Make that dream trip of yours

happen (after you've saved for it of course!). Apply for the job you think you'll never get. Branch out and try new things. Reach out and meet new people your age; they are feeling the same way you do. Experience the freedom to fail.

10. Don't compare. You will probably have a friend who is instantly successful. Making more money than they dreamed of. Enjoying their job, having fun at night, and looking like they are completely in their wheelhouse. Don't worry. Be happy for them. Your time will come. People only post the exciting stuff on social media, not the hard stuff. And that's okay. We all do it, but don't let social media fool you. It may look like everything is good and dandy for everyone else, but there's a good chance that your friends are having a hard time too. You're not alone. Your first job is not your final job. While landing the perfect job would be awesome, don't stress out about it. A first job is a first job as long for as you work there—whether it's thirty days or thirty years. There's a 99.9 percent chance you won't be at your first job for more than three years, whether you love the job or not.

Know that your future is bright. Your best years are yet to come! You may think that life will be on a slow but steady downward spiral from now on. That's not true. Imagine if you get married and have children. They're not going to give you better times than college? This is ridiculous. College was an incredible time in my life, but know that the best years are truly yet to come.

Welcome to the real world. We've been waiting for you.

NOTES

Introduction

1 Tom Ziglar, "If you aim at nothing …" *Ziglar*, June 2, 2016, accessed October 6, 2017, https://www.ziglar.com/articles/if-you-aim-at-nothing-2/.

Chapter 1

1 Joel Brown, "The Top 10 Regrets in Life by Those About to Die," *Addicted2Success*, May 26, 2016, https://addicted2success.com/success-advice/infographic-the-top-10|-regrets-in-life-by-those-about-to-die/.

2 Laurie Beth Jones, *The Path: Creating Your Mission Statement for Work and Life* (New York: Hachette Books, 2001), 9.

Chapter 5

1 Corinne J. Naden and Rose Blue, *Wilma Rudolph* (Chicago: Raintree, 2004), 7.

2 Kevin Kruse, "100 Best Quotes on Leadership," *Forbes*, October 16, 2012, accessed October 11, 2017, https://www.forbes.com/sites/kevinkruse/2012/10/16/quotes-on-leadership/#36274b642feb.

3 Michael McNew, "John Maxwell's Law of Process," *Visceral Concepts*, accessed October 11, 2017, https://www.visceralconcepts.com/john-maxwells-law-process.

4 Mark J. Warner and William F. Evans, *Inspiring Leadership: It's Not About the Power* (Boston: Pearson Custom Publishing, 2006), n.p.

5 This question was inspired by Andy Stanley.

6 Jayson DeMers, "How To Be A Leader People Want To Follow," *Business Insider*, October 16, 2014, accessed October 11, 2017, http://www.businessinsider.com/how-to-be-a-leader-people-want-to-follow-2014-10.

Chapter 6

1 "Management Chapter 11 Terms," *Quizlet*, accessed October 9, 2017, https://quizlet.com/105774669/management-chapter-11-terms-flash-cards/.

2 Ni, Preston. 2014. "How to Increase Your Emotional Intelligence - 6 Essentials." *Psychology Today*, October 5, 2014, https://www.psychologytoday.com/blog/communication-success/201410/how-increase-your-emotional-intelligence-6-essentials.

3 Gordon Tredgold, "10 Tips for Boosting Your People Skills," *Inc.*, July 21, 2016, accessed October 9, 2017, https://www.inc.com/gordon-tredgold/10-ways-to-improve-your-eq-be-a-better-lead-infographic.html.

4 Timothy Keller, *The Freedom of Self-Forgetfulness: The Path to True Christian Joy* (Leyland, England: 10Publishing, 2012), 32.

5   https://www.post-it.com/3M/en_US/post-it/ideas/articles/how-collaboration-changed
    -the-world-5-famous-partnerships.
6   https://en.wikipedia.org/wiki/Collaboration.

Chapter 7

1   "Quotes for Ben Parker," *IMDb*, accessed October 9, 2017, http://www.imdb.com/
    character/ch0001368/quotes.
2   Joe S. McIlhaney Jr. and Freda McKissic Bush, *Hooked: New Science on How Casual
    Sex is Affecting Our Children* (Chicago: Northfield Publishing, 2008), 8.
3   Tim Keller, "Money Worship," *Daily Keller*, August 4, 2017, accessed October 8,
    2017, http://dailykeller.com/money-worship.
4   These thoughts on desire were inspired by Pat Goodman.
5   J. Budziszewski, *On the Meaning of Sex* (Wilmington, Delaware: Intercollegiate
    Studies Institute, 2014), n.p.
6   Genesis 1:27–28, 31; 2:24. God created human beings male and female. This
    includes our sexual anatomy, which we use to fulfill God's command to be "fruitful
    and multiply, and fill the earth" (1:28 NASB). He calls all that he creates good, which
    makes our sexuality good. And part of marriage is becoming "one flesh," which
    means, among other things, joining together in the most intimate of acts called sex.
    This strengthens the bond between a husband and a wife.
7   Marva Dawn, *Sexual Character: Beyond Technique to Intimacy* (Grand Rapids: Wm. B.
    Eerdmans Publishing, 1993), 21.
8   Ibid, 38.
9   McIlhaney and Bush, *Hooked*, 126.
10 Eric Metaxas, "How 'soul mate' nonsense is destroying Christian marriages," *LifeSite*,
    September 28, 2015, accessed October 9, 2017, https://www.lifesitenews.com/opinio
    /how-soul-mate-nonsense-is-destroying-christian-marriages.
11 Andy Stanley, "The New Rules for Love, Sex, and Dating," *North Point Community
    Church*, May 2011, accessed October 9, 2017, http://northpoint.org/messages/the-
    new-rules-for-love-sex-and-dating.
12 Regan McMeehan, "Porn addiction destroys relationships, lives," *SFGate*, February
    22, 2010, accessed October 11, 2017, http://www.sfgate.com/health/article/Porn
    -addiction-destroys-relationships-lives-3272230.php.
13 William M. Struthers, *Wired for Intimacy: How Porn Highjacks the Male Brain 16th ed.*
    (ReadHowYouWant, 2012), 76.
14 Ibid, 11.
15 "Top Five Researched Negative Effects of Pornography," *Dr. Syras Derksen*, October
    14, 2013, accessed October 11, 2017, http://www.drsyrasderksen.com/blog/ef-
    fects-of-pornography#sthash.kdR0XCa3.dpbs.
16 Ann Tolley, "10 toxic side effects of pornography use," *FamilyShare*, accessed October
    11, 2017, https://familyshare.com/394/10-toxic-side-effects-of-pornography-use.
17 "This Is Your Brain on Porn," *Christianity Today*, accessed October 11, 2017, http://

www.christianitytoday.com/pastors/2010/spring/yourbrainporn.html.

Chapter 8

1 "11 Facts About Global Poverty," *DoSomething.org*, accessed October 9, 2017, https://www.dosomething.org/us/facts/11-facts-about-global-poverty.

2 John C. Bogle, *Enough: True Measures of Money, Business, and Life* (Hoboken: Wiley & Sons, Inc., 2009), 1.

3 Brigitt Hauck, "Could This Much Money Make You Happier at Work?" *Real Simple*, accessed October 9, 2017, https://www.realsimple.com/work-life/money/salary-happiness.

4 Rick Hendrickson, "Earn all you can, Save all you can, and Give all you can," *The United Methodist Church of Greater New Jersey*, October 5, 2015, accessed October 9, 2017, https://www.gnjumc.org/earn-all-you-can-save-all-you-can-and-give-all-you-can.

5 Bryan Rex, in an email (August 15, 2017), used with permission.

6 Kerri Anne Renzulli, "The Costly Career Mistake Millennials Are Making," *Time*, May 14, 2015, accessed October 9, 2017, http://time.com/money/3855869/millennials-first-job-salary.

Chapter 9

1 J. D. Roth, "How to Build a Better Budget," *Fox Business*, May 3, 2011, accessed October 9, 2017, http://www.foxbusiness.com/features/2011/05/03/build-better-budget.html.

2 Warren Buffett, as cited by Paul A. Merriman, "The Genius of Warren Buffett in 23 Quotes," MarketWatch, August 19, 2015, accessed October 19, 2017, http://www.marketwatch.com/story/the-genius-of-warren-buffett-in-23-quotes-2015-08-19.

3 "Biden's Remarks on McCain's Policies," *New York Times*, September 15, 2008, accessed October 9, 2017, http://www.nytimes.com/2008/09/15/us/politics/15text-biden.html.

Chapter 10

1 "Compound Interest," *Investopedia*, accessed October 9, 2017, http://www.investopedia.com/terms/c/compoundinterest.asp.

2 Maggie McGrath, "63% of Americans Don't Have Enough Savings to Cover a $500 Emergency," *Forbes*, January 6, 2016, accessed October 9, 2017, https://www.forbes.com/sites/maggiemcgrath/2016/01/06/63-of-americans-dont-have-enough-savings-to-cover-a-500-emergency/#1e5d48f64e0d.

Chapter 11

1 Pablo Torre, "How (and Why) Athletes Go Broke," *Sports Illustrated*, March 23, 2009, accessed October 9, 2017, https://www.si.com/vault/2009/03/23/105789480/how-and-why-athletes-go-broke.

Chapter 12

1 Stepp, Erin. 2017. "Your Driving Costs 2017." AAA News Room, August 23, 2017, http://newsroom.aaa.com/auto/your-driving-costs.

Chapter 15

1 "Quarterly Report on Household Debt and Credit," https://www.newyorkfed.org /medialibrary/interactives/householdcredit/data/pdf/HHDC_2017Q2.pdf.

Chapter 16

1 http://www.apa.org/monitor/oct01/multitask.aspx.
2 https://news.stanford.edu/2009/08/24/multitask-research-study-082409.
3 Travis Bradberry, https://www.forbes.com/sites/travisbradberry/2014/10/08 /multitasking-damages-your-brain-and-career-new-studies-suggest/#28d737e856ee.
4 Jaroldeen Asplundh Edwards, *The Daffodil Principle: One Woman, Two Hands, One Bulb at a Time* (Salt Lake City: Shadow Mountain, 2004), n.p..

Chapter 18

1 Nicole Spector, "2017 New Year's Resolutions: The Most Popular and How to Stick to Them," *NBC News*, January 1, 2017, accessed October 10, 2017, https://www. nbcnews.com/business/consumer/2017-new-year-s-resolutions-most-popular-how -stick-them-n701891.
2 John Stonestreet and G. Shane Morris, "Where Is God in the Storms?" *Break-Point*, September 19, 2017, accessed October 11, 2017, http://www.breakpoint. org/2017/09/breakpoint-god-storms.

Chapter 19

1 Truett Cathy, *It's Easier to Succeed Than to Fail* (Nashville: Thomas Nelson, 1989), 188–92.
2 Anonymous.
3 Gerald Ford, thirty-eighth president of the United States.

Appendix 1

1 Cal Newport, *How to Win at College: Surprising Secrets for Success from the Country's Top Students* (New York: Three Rivers Press, 2005).
2 Timothy Dalrymple, "An Open Letter to a College Freshman," *Patheos*, September 1, 2011, accessed October 11, 2017, http://www.patheos.com/blogs/philosophical fragments/2011/09/01/an-open-letter-to-a-college-freshman/#comment-7862.

Appendix 2

1 Joanna Hyatt, "Talking Twentysomethings with Paul Angone," *VerilyMag*, August 30, 2013, accessed October 11, 2017, https://verilymag.com/2013/08/talking-twenty somethings-with-paul-angone.

ACKNOWLEDGMENTS

From Josh Burnette:

Adulting 101 would not have been possible without the support of the most important people in my life: my family. To my stunning wife, Katie, thank you for spending countless hours reading, rereading, and editing this manuscript. You were pregnant and gave birth to our son, Brody, during the process of writing this book, so we've had a lot going on, but you've never wavered in your love and support for me in this endeavor.

To my children, Lyla and Brody, this book is for you. I hope one day you will be prepared to launch into the real world with confidence and excitement.

To my parents, Brian and Kim, you were my first mentors and taught me so much of what I needed to know to survive beyond the walls of your home. Thank you for being intentional and loving me even when I'm sure I drove you crazy.

To Chick-fil-A, my life would look a whole lot different without you. Chick-fil-A was my first job, how I met my wife, and how I provide for my family. I can honestly say that I don't know where I would be without this company.

The Chick-fil-A family is made up of many parts. To the Cathy family, thank you for taking a risk on a twenty-four-year-old kid and giving me a chance to prove myself as an Owner/Operator. Your family has been the greatest business partner that I could have ever hoped for.

To my Chick-fil-A team members, past and present, thank you for teaching me every single day. I am honored to work with each of you. You were the main motivation for creating *Adulting 101*.

To the team at BroadStreet Publishing, thank you for taking a flyer on two completely unknown authors. You have invested time, money, and a whole lot of energy into making this dream a reality.

Lastly, to Pete Hardesty, for mentoring me when I was a knucklehead college kid and showing me how to succeed in life after college. Your impact from over a decade ago has helped to pave the way for me on my journey as a father, husband, and business owner. You made this book idea into way more than just a Word document and into something that we hope will impact many lives for the better.

From Pete Hardesty:

To my mom and dad. You were the first ones who taught me about a life well-lived and how to love others. You showed me how to "adult" and set me up for success. I am eternally grateful to you and for you. Also, thank you for always proofreading and providing feedback on such short notice. I love you.

To my sister, Julnanee, and my brother-in-law, Meathead Shawny. The ideal sister doesn't exi…Wha…actually, she does. And she's my sister. I love you. Thank you for picking such a great husband too, who feels more like a brother than a brother-in-law.

To my nieces, Hales and Lils. You are the most incredible girls in the universe. God has huge things in store for your lives. You are both world-changers. Love you more than you know.

To my "life admin," Jen Valliere. Thank you for your patience throughout this process and for your willingness to go the second mile.

To YoungLife. You are an organization that has changed my life (and many others). I am grateful for the countless opportunities for adventure and abundant life that you have provided. I am honored to be involved with such a phenomenal group of people.

To all my James Madison University grads. My life will never be the same. Thank you for teaching me how to dream big and the importance of every kid. This book is written in hopes that you will "adult" to your full potential.

To Aimee Kessick and Jess DeMayo Mann. Thank you for reviewing the entire book and giving us invaluable feedback about how to tell the story better.

To Dave Barbetta and Bryan Rex. You guys are financial gurus. Thank you for the great help with the financial chapters.

Thank you to these unsung heroes working with young people who contributed to the appendices: Stefan Wiltz, Brian Griffith, Nathan Gunn, Josh Goodman, Matt Bouknight, Bige Philip Bowling, Will Cox, Heather Beam, Derek Walne, Lou Chicchetto, Sara Cummings, Caroline Heese, Jake Johnson.

To BroadStreet Publishing. Thank you for the tremendous amount of time, energy, patience, and wisdom you have spent on us. We are grateful for you. Thanks also to Joy Groblebe (and her dog Blantons) for connecting us with BroadStreet.

To my mentors. Much of this book is based on your wisdom. You have made me who I am. I thank God every day for you. Pat Goodman, Reverend Ralph Gates, Jack Birsch, Scott Hamilton, Danny O'Brien, Chuck Reinhold, Win Levis, Pastor Merle and Pastor Peter, Jerry and Holly Leachman (and many others).

To Josh "Chick" Burnette. This book would not exist without you. Thank you for taking a risk and asking me to partner with you on this project. What a joy it's been to see the student become the teacher! You have taught me so much these last two years, and I am grateful for your deep friendship. Thanks for keeping the vision in front of us to help people and change lives for the better. You certainly have changed mine. For the better.

ABOUT THE AUTHORS

 **JOSH BURNETTE** is a husband, dad, business owner, and author who currently resides in Little Rock, Arkansas.

Originally from Virginia Beach, Virginia, he started working for Chick-fil-A as a team member when he was barely old enough to see over the counter. He received his bachelor's degree in business management from James Madison University in 2009 (Go Dukes!). Throughout college, he served as a Young Life leader for a local high school, and his passion for mentoring young people began. After graduating, he went to work fulltime for a Young Life camp in Buena Vista, Colorado. He decided to come back to Chick-fil-A to combine his loves for business and working with young people. He served as the owner/operator of a mall restaurant for two years and currently leads a free-standing restaurant employing over one hundred people in Little Rock.

Josh is a certified speaker with SCORRE workshops and recently enjoyed the opportunity to be the keynote speaker for Verizon Wireless. In his free time, he enjoys reading, traveling, volunteering on several boards in the community, and snowboarding.

Josh is married to his gorgeous wife Katie, and they have two young children, Lyla and Brody.

PETE HARDESTY currently serves as the Young Life college divisional coordinator in the Eastern Division. He moved to the Washington, D.C. area from the friendly city of Harrisonburg, Virginia.

Pete grew up in Baltimore, Maryland, and graduated from the University of Virginia where he was pre-med with the emphasis on "pre." He then joined the staff of Young Life in Virginia Beach, where he served for seven years before moving to Harrisonburg in 2004. After being the area director for Young Life in Harrisonburg for eight years, Pete transitioned to start Young Life College at James Madison University in 2012. Pete loves being around college students even though they make him feel old. He crammed his three years of grad school into seventeen and finally received his Master of Divinity from Reformed Theological Seminary in 2014.

A passion for the Middle East has inspired Pete to lead Holy Land trips for the last ten years, with a focus on serving Palestinian kids in the West Bank. He is a frequent international keynote speaker with experience in such places as Asia, Africa, the Middle East, the Caribbean, and places all over the US, speaking to groups as big as four thousand. He is a speaker coach with SCORRE workshops and loves helping people become excellent communicators.

Pete has been working with young people for twenty-five years. They are still his favorite. He loves people and creating environments where they can thrive and achieve their potential. His two nieces are the apple of his eye.

You can connect with Pete, ask him to speak, or read more of his work at NoRedos.com.